TAKING IT TO THE STREETS

A PASSION FOR A PURPOSE

Dr. Ray Hampton

Ray Hampton 2/21/22

ISBN: 978-1-7368015-9-8

Unless otherwise expressed, all quotations and references must be permitted by Authors. All scripture references from NKJ and NIV Bibles.

Cover Design:
Business Startup & Marketing Solutions LLC and JWG Publishing House.

Published by

Printed in the United States of America.

ISBN: 978-1-7368015-9-8

Unless otherwise expressed, all quotations and references must be permitted by Authors. All scripture references from NKJ and NIV Bibles.

Cover Design:
Business Startup & Marketing Solutions LLC and JWG Publishing House.

Published by

Printed in the United States of America.

Endorsements

My dear friend Ray, I want to take a moment to tell you how proud I am of the great work that you are doing. I know what you are doing is really hard work, but for over the last 25 years and counting you have really stuck with it. My sons' Pastor Matthew Barnett's book, titled "The Church That Never Sleeps" states that the Seattle Dream Center was one of many Dream Centers that started as an extension of the LA Dream Center. Over the years you have been to several of our Pastors and Leaders school hosted at Phoenix and the LA Dream Center. Many of the Seattle Dream Center outreaches. such as Feeding the hungry and homeless that are living on the streets of Seattle, Adopt-A-Block, Sidewalk Sunday School, Backpack and School supply giveaways and of course your annual Christmas toy giveaway were over 100,000 toys have been gifted to children just to name a few, have made a tremendous difference in the lives of thousands of people. I sure love you and admire you my dear friend. Keep up the good work.

Pastor Tommy Barnett

Dr Ray Hampton III embodies the title of this book, "Taking it to the Streets." Anyone that knows Dr Raymond Hampton III knows that the book could simply be titled "Dr Raymond Hampton III, The True Definition of Outreach Ministry." The Body of Christ is blessed that he can share his vast experience and his teaching from years of expertly navigating successful street ministries.

For over 30 years, I have seen him achieved phenomenal results from street to street, block to block, and city to city. This book will show you how to impact those outside the church walls in an easy-to-understand way that is consistently achievable. He has mentored and taught through his outreach classes and national speaking engagements hundreds of believers on how to be epic and unstoppable in outreach ministry.

If you want to change your life and expand your ministry, invest, and purchase this book for yourself and other leaders. It will quickly make you a doer of the Word and not just a hearer only, James 1:22. I emphatically recommend this book to help you fulfill the great commission with insightful ways to reap a harvest of souls and keep reaching a new harvest of souls, season after season.

Bishop Craig Jackson
King of Glory Worldwide Ministry, Founder and Bishop

Dr. Ray Hampton Is the most anointed and gifted evangelist that I have ever known. I believe that He is the authority and expert on how to develop a powerful, lasting, and effective outreach ministry in your church. Personally, I've known Dr Hampton for well over 25 years and during that time he's been nonstop doing the work of the lord, he has had an incredible hunger, thirst and desire to see the lost saved, to see the hungry fed, the sick healed and the less fortunate blessed especially with his dynamic toys give away every Christmas season for hundreds of thousands precious little children. I believe if you are ready to study the heart of a true modern day Holy Ghost filled Evangelist, and if you're ready to have a more effective outreach program in your ministry, then by reading this book you are in for the journey of your life!

Dr. Jason Martin Sr
Kingdom Church International

I honor the work of Dr. Ray Hampton and how God use him in last 25 years plus in evangelism for Kingdom of God. I know him for over two decades we both have been encouraging one another's to live transformation by the gospel. I would recommend that you read this book it will bless you and expand your vision in reaching the lost. Study his on personal life on this journey will increase your faith plus give you a sense of Divine Purpose and Assignment for your life. This book will change your life forever.

Blessings to you all.
Bishop David Horn
Harvest Celebration Program

Dr. Ray Hampton is a standout in every way. He has been a huge asset to our team during his time here at the Emergency Feeding Program of Seattle/King County. Dr. Hampton has brought a great deal of knowledge to our organization and is very respectful of our goals and mission to provide sustainable healthy food to the greater King County community. He has developed and implemented the Save Our Streets (SOS) program providing food to our most vulnerable, the homeless over the past two years. In his efforts Dr. Hampton has been a beacon in the King County community for more than 30 years providing food, clothing, and preaching the word of GOD. It is my honor to provide this note of gratitude to such an honorable and genuine man. It has been a pleasure to collaborate with him over the past 9 years and pray there will be more to come.

Glenn Turner
Executive Director
Emergency Feeding Program
Seattle/King County

I have never seen a minister of the Gospel with so much compassion for the lost soul. Started his ministry on the street of Seattle and now traveling in many states of America preaching actively as the Holy Spirit leads him. I take my hat off to this man of God. This new book " Taking it to the Street" is a great book for every Christian to read and get the kind of compassion that Dr. Ray Hampton has.

Bishop Israel Sanoy
Founder and Pastor of Love Fellowship Church International

"Great evangelism is developed in the crucible of life. Bishop Ray Hampton has studied and lived evangelism. I can say without any reservation that Bishop Hampton has the gift of teaching people and leaders how to maximize their ability to evangelize. This book will give you the living example from Bishop Hampton's life on how he developed this gift and the practical steps to grow in your evangelism journey."

All the best,
Tony Morris

Dr. Ray Hampton offers an exquisite piece of work as he takes us on his intriguing journey of ministry for the past 25 years. He does a masterful job of encouraging the believer to stay committed to the assignment God has entrusted to you. Over the years I have witnessed first-hand Hampton's dedication to the Kingdom, from adept evangelism trainings to his passion for feeding the hungry and less fortunate. I commend this book to you and believe it will enhance your ability to do the work of the Kingdom.

Bishop Reggie C. Witherspoon Sr. D.D.
Senior Pastor Mt. Calvary Christian Center Church of God in Christ
Prelate Washington Northwest Ecclesiastical Jurisdiction

I have been acquainted with Dr. Ray Hampton for over 35 years and his light continues to shine bright! Our partnership has progressed; his ministry has provided hope around the world helping to transform the lives of thousands. This book will definitely inspire pastors, evangelists, and laity!

Bishop Alvin C. Moore, Sr.
Washington State Jurisdiction, Prelate
Church Of God In Christ, Inc.

As the Senior Pastor of Vision Church and Director of Vision Hope Center, I use Dr. Raymond Hampton's books to pour into our leadership team, which have helped to turn them into out of the box thinkers in the areas of outreach! This body of work needs to be in leadership's hands!

Pastor Donald Moody

Dr. Ray Hampton is a voice crying in a wilderness of fear and uncertainty as to how we take the compelling Gospel of Jesus Christ to the unchurched. Amidst division and confusion in the body of Christ, His passion and methods present a clear message to believers who seeks to connect the Gospel to the

Streets. To those looking to remain true to the call and speak with conviction and clarity, this work is a necessity in every library.

Bishop CT Wells,
Senior Pastor Emmanuel Church, Portland, Oregon

"I have known Dr. Ray Hampton since 1991 when he was simply known as Minister Ray Hampton. I recognized his commitment to the ministry as he faithfully drove a 35-foot church bus, a repurposed school bus, from Everett to Seattle Washington every Sunday. Eventually, he began to minister on the streets within the local community where he focused on feeding and clothing the homeless and providing gifts and backpacks to children".

Dr. Hampton is approachable, down to earth, focused, and faithful to God's call on his life -- to take it to the streets!

Pastor Ronnie G Parker
Word of Life Church of God Renton WA

Bishop Raymond Hampton was ordained as a Pastor at the then Power House Church of God in Christ in December 1989. He served as a faithful minister in the early 1980s until he left to begin his ministry in the 1990's. Bishop Hampton and his family were faithful, dependable, and dedicated to the vision of the church. He had a passion for helping those in need and traveled from the city of Everett to Seattle ((about forty miles) as the church's bus driver to ensure those who needed transportation could attend church. In his current Kingdom work as head of a feeding program, he continues to touch the lives of so many through his food distribution ministry. He without fail serves the needs of others through providing weekly grab and go boxes of food to ensure families have basic substance. His community service outreach efforts uplifts and supports the many families he touches. It is with great honor and gratitude that I write this letter of acknowledgement. Bishop Hampton is doing the work of Christ, serving those in need. His dedicated service and unselfish love are truly a blessing.

Pastor Henry A. Jenkins
Miracle Temple Church of God in Christ

Dedication

I would like to dedicate this book to my wife Julia and our children Trenecsia, Catrena, Ramon, Michael, Terrance, Tyrrell, and Brittany. Also, to the amazing congregation and staff of the Seattle International Church and Dream Center. Because of your prayers and support this book was able to be published.

Table of Contents

Chapter 1

"A PASSION FOR A PURPOSE"

"A lot of people are trying to find their purpose, but I never found my purpose until I was obedient to my passion."

Dr. Ray Hampton

WHAT IS PASSION?

"To be passionate is to have an intense emotional excitement. It is to be enthusiastic, have a continued zeal, strong desire and feeling towards something. When you are passionate about something you will have a craving and stirring up within yourself".

How can an individual find their passion?

It frustrates you or brings excitement to you. If you cannot find your passion within yourself; maybe what you have been called to has not been created at this time.

"Passion and Purpose is going to be the Key to your success in your life."

1

The words *Passion and Purpose* are both important and easy to use them interchangeably. I believe that there's a difference between the two words.

What is passion?

When you're passionate about something; it will always bring you fulfillment in your life. A true passion for something drives you to a purpose that pulls you, to the thing that you're passionate about. Your drive is your movement, momentum, and Journey to the destination that you are being pulled to.

When you're passionate about something, it means that you can spend all day doing it and by the end of the day when you lay your head on a pillow you feel fulfilled just to wake up the next morning and work your passion again. Your passion will also bring you endless joy and contentment.

I want to share an important fact with you before you read any further. Everything that you're passionate about might not be your purpose. I was passionate about football and wanted to do it for university, but it was not my purpose. I have played the bass guitar for years and had a passion to play in a band or group that was going to be known across the world, but that wasn't my purpose. As you continue to read, "Taking it to the Streets" a passion for a purpose; you are going to find out how I found my passion for purpose, and I believe you're going to find out your passion as well. Guess what, it's not lost; it's already in you trying to come out.

WHAT IS PURPOSE?

"A person may have many ideas concerning God's plan for his life, but only the designs of God's purpose will succeed in the end."

Proverbs 19:21 TPT

There are many plans in a man's heart: It is in the nature of men (and women) to plan and prepare for the future. Some of the plans may be wise and some may be foolish.

Nevertheless, the Lord's counsel will stand: Man makes his plans, and he should. Yet every plan should be made with an appreciation of God's overall wisdom, work, and will.

Your purpose is your "reason for being." It is the culmination of your passions, and the impact you want to make on the world, which is why it drives you forward and keeps you motivated, fulfilled, happy, and of course, confident.

"So, let's not allow ourselves to get fatigued doing good. At the right time we will harvest a good crop if we don't give up, or quit. Right now, therefore, every time we get the chance, let us work for the benefit of all, starting with the people closest to us in the community of faith."

Galatians 6:9-10 MSG

So, remember even when you're working within your passion, some days and nights might seem difficult, but you will always see a harvest if you don't quit. I must be very honest

3

with you, over the last 30 plus years that I have been serving and empowering others, there has been hundreds (okay thousands) of times that I wanted to give up and quit. I did not want to travel across the states, did not want to go back to Africa, no more annual events throughout the community, city, and state such as feeding the hungry and homeless, toy, backpack school supplies giveaway, shoes to children, gas giveaway and the list goes on. But there was just a drive in me to always get to a location to help someone. It is important that you do not ever let anyone, or anything detour you from what you're passionate about. Even though some days it might feel as though your passion has been delayed; it will never be denied. If you continue your movement, you will not turn into a monument. Never look back and if you do, I'll guarantee you will get stuck.

> *"I'm not saying that I have this all together, that I have it made. But I am well on my way, reaching out for Christ, who has so wondrously reached out for me. Friends don't get me wrong: By no means do I count myself an expert in all of this, but I've got my eye on the goal, where God is beckoning us onward—to Jesus. I'm off and running, and I'm not turning back."*

Philippians 3:12-14 MSG

If I have not given up or quit in over 30 years neither should you! God started this passionate work within me and within you, whatever that maybe, so stop doubting what you were made to do, get ready set and go until you reach the finish line.

> *"There has never been the slightest doubt in my mind that the God who started this great work in you would keep at it and bring it to a flourishing finish on the very day Christ Jesus appears."*

Philippians 1:6 MSG

You are called to do something great and whatever you were told to do, just do it.

> *2 "On the third day there was a wedding at Cana of Galilee, and the mother of Jesus was there; ² and both Jesus and His disciples were invited to the wedding. ³ When the wine was all gone, the mother of Jesus said to Him, "They have no more wine." ⁴ Jesus said to her, "[Dear] woman, what is that to you and to Me? My time [to act and to be revealed] has not yet come." ⁵ His mother said to the servants,* **"Whatever He says to you, do it."**

Look what happened next after the disciples followed the instructions that were given by Jesus.

> *Now there were six stone waterpots set there for the Jewish custom of purification (ceremonial washing), containing twenty or thirty gallons each. ⁷ Jesus said to the servants, "Fill the waterpots with water." So, they filled them up to the brim. ⁸ Then He said to them, "Draw some out now and take it to the headwaiter [of the banquet]." So, they took it to him. ⁹ And when the headwaiter tasted the water which had turned into wine, not knowing where it came from (though the servants who had drawn the water knew) he called the bridegroom…"*

John 2:6-9 AMP

I want you to pause for a moment and imagine what your church, ministry, business, or life would be like if you decided to stay focus and listen to the instructions given to you by Jesus. Stop procrastinating and start working your passion; it did not come from you, it came to you, so it can be worked through you for the benefit of you and others. No one can stop you, stay focused on the one that gave you the gift. God has not changed His mind about what He Has called you to do. You might change your mind, but God has not changed His mind about what He called you to do.

"For the gifts and the calling of God are irrevocable [for He does not withdraw what He has given, nor does He change His mind about those to whom He gives His grace or to whom He sends His call."

Romans 11:29 AMP

Your passion and purpose to which you have been called to cannot be cancelled or reversed. Stop trying to figure out what God has already worked out in you; all you need to do is walk it out.

Now, let us talk about purpose. What is purpose? Purpose to your passion is like gasoline in an automobile, it is the source that fuels you to arrive consistently to your place and purpose of passion every day. For over 30 years my life was a consistent distribution center by colliding with others that are in need or at a disadvantage. I have been able to make an impact to thousands of lives through-out the states and

6

internationally. One major point I really want you to understand is the greater your collision is to your passion the greater the impact will be. It's not going to be in your own strength that causes a great impact in others, it's going to be His strength connected with you and through you to achieve the calling you were born and chosen to do. You have been empowered to fulfill a purpose in life, so keep your peace, stay confident and go achieve your passion.

> *11 For I know the plans and thoughts that I have for you,' says the LORD, 'plans for peace and well-being and not for disaster, to give you a future and a hope."*

Jeremiah 29:11 AMP

Your purpose, whatever it is, must be something that positively impacts others.

You can use your passion(s) to help you find your purpose.

Do you know the difference between your purpose and passion?

Every day you awake to accomplish your passion and at the end of the day, do you still feel like you missed something, or that someone did not get served? Do you know that the passion that you currently have is a desire or strong emotion towards something? Do you also know that you can like something and not be passionate about it, such as athletics, music, food or etc.

You should never have to search for your passion, why? Because it is the thing that you think about all the time. I did not have to search for my passion as I stated earlier. My passion did not drive me to do the many outreaches that have been accomplished over the last 30 plus years, my passion has continually pushed me while my purpose has pulled me day after day. When you are passionate about something you must embrace it. I am not saying you should quit your job to pursue a new career, but love what you love and make time for it in your life. There's 24 hours in a day, make sure that you use it wisely, remember that your time is valuable, so whoever you connect to is very important. Connect with people that are going in the same direction as you especially when it's concerning your passion. Don't waste time because you cannot get that time back!

The message of your Passion can always remain the same, but your methods, how you relate the message can change. Your passions can be for a moment or stay with you your entire life. To discover your passion, you must pay attention to yourself, because your passion stems from your expressions. The following are some questions to ask yourself, so you will know what your true passion is:

- ⊙ Is it bigger than you?
- ⊙ What are you willing to give up to achieve your passion?

- What job would you work without pay?
- Does your passion and purpose solve a problem(s)?
- Is your passion and purpose something people need or want?
- What's your niche?
- What frustrates you?

Through-out the years, thousands of individuals have approached me and have consistently asked me this particular question, "How do you keep doing all these outreaches, consistently every year? My answers are always the same, "This is one of my major assignments in life and I'm Grace to do it." If you see an airplane on a freeway that might be a problem, but when it's in the air the plane is in its Grace zone. My question to you is, what are you currently doing in life? is it hard? Do you like doing it? If that's the case, you're probably not in your Grace zone. Remember, when you do whatever Jesus tells you to do the Harvest of manifestations will always come!

> *"Then the Lord turned to him and said, "Go with the strength you have, and rescue Israel from the Midianites. I am sending you!"*

Judges 6:14 NLT

In verse 14, God said to Gideon, "go in your strength", in other words, function in your Grace Zone. Just like Gideon, you have a grace zone. Which are your strengths, talent, or special ability. Remember, when you are working in your Grace zone, it will always look hard to most people, but for you it's easy. Why? Because you are Grace to do it. In other words, you were born for the assignment that has been given to you. Did you know that God created you from the foundation of the earth for a purpose and that when you were born from your mother's womb, He already had a plan for you?

"Trust GOD from the bottom of your heart; don't try to figure out everything on your own. Listen for GOD 's voice in everything you do, everywhere you go; He's the one who will keep you on track. Do not assume that you know it all."

Proverbs 3:5-6 MSG

When you have discovered your passion, the next thing is to find out what your purpose is, so that you can begin to channel your passion in the direction of your purpose.

Purpose precedes passion, though we often get to discover our passions first because they are expressive. Your passions can be a clue to help you figure out what your purpose is.

You can have a lot of Passions, but before you start you should first sit down and clearly hear your vision, write your vision, read your vision, and then run with the vision. Once you create a blueprint for your passion, it will help you effectively define your purpose. I remember in my younger years I would jump from passion to passion without finishing anything that I had started.

There were many times throughout the years that I really had no direction until I realized that having a mentor who had been on the same path that I was getting ready to Journey will be very helpful. I strongly suggest to you that whatever assignment that you own, such as Feeding the hungry, providing clothes, backpacks and school supplies, thanksgiving meals, Christmas toys, tutoring, nursing home, Jail and prison, marketplace business, Pastoral, teaching, evangelism, outreach or (say what you are currently doing) Just to name a few. Whatever it is, just make sure that you're ALL IN! It reminds me of a story about the cow, chicken, and pig. They all got together and had a conversation and decided to have a feast. The cow spoke to the chicken and pig and said, "I will bring all the milk," the chicken spoke to the cow and pig and said, "I'll bring all the eggs." The pig was so excited about the feast that he wanted to bring something as well, so he shouted out with a real loud voice and said, "I'll bring all the bacon." The pig's excitement didn't last long because he quickly realized that he was ALL IN. The point I want you to get from the story is, whatever your passion and purpose is; you must be ALL IN!

I needed my purpose to turn my passions into something sustainable and purposeful in helping people. So, which comes first? Passion generally comes before purpose. A passion is what gets you started, and a purpose is what keeps you going. Passion and purpose are both important for you to have a great impact in your community, city, state, and the world. If you have passion with no Purpose or purpose with no passion you will always end up feeling like you are lacking something. Passion generally comes before purpose. A passion is what gets you started, and a purpose is what keeps you going. Passion is about emotions, the motivation and what makes you feel good because you're doing what you love to do. Purpose is the reason, or the why behind what we do, primarily for others. Where passion can be all over the place, wild and exciting, purpose is much more focused. When I started preaching and feeding the hungry on the street corner, there was no social media such as Instagram, Facebook, Twitter, websites or cell phones to get the word out. It was only the work and words of others that scaled the ministry and this led to the expansion and enlargement of the evangelism and outreach ministry that is now through-out the United States as well as internationally.

Each One Reach One Philosophy

"Philosophy is the general principles or a particular system of a field of knowledge for the conduct of life"

PASSION - When you are passionate for someone or something, you will have an intense emotional excitement. You will always have a continued zeal, strong desire, feeling toward something or someone which causes a craving and stirring up within yourself.

PERSISTENCE – Your persistency will show your patients toward a certain goal even when you are faced with opposition and going through adversity; you refuse to give up, cave in or quit because of the endurance with in you to bear the pain without flinching.

PRODUCTIVITY – Fertilization will always bring fruit, because of your productivity. It is the act of producing or the giving and putting out your effort to see an increasing product to realization.

PRODUCE – To produce means that you have given life to something or someone and now you have a cause and effect of a product. The product is the result of your productivity and will cause birth to a production of something else.

PASSION = BELIEF SYSTEM

- Focus on the one and not the thousand
- Get around people that have your answer and not your problems
- If you are not net-working you're not-working
- Proper planning prevents poor performance
- Do what you have to do, so you can do what you need to do

PERSISTENCE = EFFECTIVENESS

- Practice is not just perfect, it's permanent
- Goals without dates are dreams
- The result of labor is favor
- How can you lead and teach what you don't know?

PRODUCTIVITY = CONFIDENCE & TRUST

- Be an asset not a liability
- Work smarter not harder
- Do the right thing because it's the right thing to do
- Don't give up
- Stay motivated

PRODUCE = SUCCESS – *"Which is measured by a transformed life"*

THE "TATOR" FAMILY

1. **COMMENTATOR** – This individual always asks, "What happened?" They rarely show up at planned events and when they are in attendance, they never do anything, but talk.

2. **SPECTATOR** – This individual "always watch things happen", they always see problems throughout the community, but never provide an answer for the problem.

3. **NON-PARTICPATOR** – This individual "always let things happen", they are physically at community meetings, but are mentally thinking about something else.

4. **IRRITATOR** – This individual represents all the above, they are always frustrating everyone and they are a huge liability instead of an asset.

5. **PARTICIPATOR** – This individual "makes things happen", they will always finish what they started.

THE SYSTEM

A system is a set of organs in the body with a common structure or function. The following scripture shows the value and importance of a born-again believer in Christ.

12 "For as the body is one and has many members, but all the members of that one body, being many, are one body, so also is Christ. 13 For by one Spirit we were all baptized into one body—whether Jews or Greeks, whether slaves or free—and have all been made to drink [a]into one Spirit. 14 For in fact the body is not one member but many. 15 If the foot should say, "Because I am not a hand, I am not of the body," is it therefore not of the body? 16 And if the ear should say, "Because I am not an eye, I am not of the body," is it therefore not of the body? 17 If the whole body were an eye, where would be the hearing? If the whole were hearing, where would be the smelling? 18 But now God has set the members, each one of them, in the body just as He pleased. 19 And if they were all one member, where would the body be?

20 But now indeed there are many members, yet one body. 21 And the eye cannot say to the hand, "I have no need of you"; nor again the head to the feet, "I have no need of you." 22 No, much rather, those members of the body which seem to be weaker are necessary. 23 And those members of the body which we think to be less honorable, on these we bestow greater honor; and our unpresentable parts have greater modesty, 24 but our presentable parts have no need. But God composed the body, having given greater honor to that part which lacks it, 25 that there should be no schism in the body, but that the members should have the same care for one another. 26 And if one member suffers, all the members suffer with it; or if one member is honored, all the members rejoice with it.

27 Now you are the body of Christ, and members individually. 28 And God has appointed these in the church: first apostles, second prophets, third teachers, after that miracles, then gifts of healings, helps, administrations, varieties of tongues. 29 Are all apostles? Are all prophets? Are all teachers? Are all workers of miracles? 30 Do all have gifts of healings? Do all speak with tongues? Do all interpret?"

1 Corinthians 12:12-30 NKJV

THE GUIDE

A guide is a general word and is something that will help you get to your destination. Guidelines are located within a guide that will give more specific directions for the purpose of leading the follower which is the believer in Christ. The bible is your guide and the scriptures are the guidelines that you follow in order to reach your goals, so that you will be able to live a successful life.

GUIDING PRINCIPLES

Guiding principles are different from core values because it causes an individual to action. If the course of actions is unclear it will cause stagnation to the individual that is un-focused, but to the organization as a whole.

EACH ONE REACH ONE GUIDING PRINCIPLES

1. Effective
2. Friendly
3. Passionate
4. Persistence
5. Productivity
6. Empower
7. Equip

WHAT ARE CORE VALUES

Core values are foundational beliefs of a person or organization. Core values will dictate the behavior and decision making that could have a negative or positive affect in the actions of the guiding principles. Core values will also help you build a solid foundation so that the guide will be clear and the guiding principles can be followed. Core values should be easy to communicate.

SEVEN CORE VALUES

1. Prayer
2. Love God
3. Love People
4. Connect with Community
5. Integrity
6. Evangelism
7. Discipleship

AIM FOCUS
WHY, WHAT AND HOW

Having a clear vision is one of the most important things you can do to make sure that there will be no barrier blockers that will hinder growth in your church or ministry. As a leader, you need to communicate mission (why) which is your assignment that is generic, and vision (why) which is the ability to think about or plan the future with wisdom and imagination. In other words, it's specific, so people can understand the why behind the what. When your mission (why) is clear, you will always know your strategy (how) and then you will effectively be able to talk about the programs (what) of your church or ministry.

Many leaders start creating and leading programs and then look for ways to justify the reasons why they are doing the programs. If your church or ministry isn't growing, don't start with your programs (what) or even your strategy (how). Start with the mission (why) and vision (why). Even though your mission (why) might be clear, there are still many people that get stuck in the strategies (how)which ultimately affects the programs (what) that you can provide to your community and city. My goal as an evangelist and outreach coach is to empower your mission (why) with your programs (what) with showing you strategies (how) your church and or ministry can grow. "Most leaders cannot effectively do what they are called to do, because they don't fully understand the assignment they have been called to.

If your church isn't growing, don't start with your programs (what) or even your strategy (how). Start with the mission (why) and vision (why). Most plants grow to the size of the pot that it's planted in, but when you transplant that same plant into a larger pot, it will begin to grow bigger. Church structure is the same, your structure can limit and hinder the growth of your church. Ironically, both ends of the leadership spectrum can hinder growth. If the leader does everything and doesn't develop leaders, the pastor is like the small pot. That's why creating a leadership team and raising up leaders is so important. If there are too many leaders, committees and levels of leadership, decision-making is slowed down and confusion takes over. If your church is not growing spiritually or physically, it could be because your time, energy and resources are dedicated to many things. More ministries, and programs will not cause healthy growth, if anything, it's very unhealthy for the church and the individuals. What you need is ultimate quality growth not only quantity growth, but remember, you can have both. Why? Because quality will always produce quantity. Start doing fewer annual events so that you can start to focus actively on weekly or monthly evangelism and outreach events throughout your community and city. You might not need to start something new, but you need to stop something now!

Chapter 2

BUILDING A CULTURE OF EVANGELISM

I formerly owned a restaurant called Hamptons Restaurant for a few years. It was normally opened for breakfast and lunch only. Leading a staff of fifteen people that comprised waitresses, waiters, cooks and managers, I learned a lot of things about being a restaurateur (owner of a restaurant), but there is one lesson that always stands out which is, "If it doesn't happen in the Kitchen, it's not going to flow into the dining room. This means, the customers will ultimately be affected perhaps to the point that they probably will not return to Hamptons restaurant. A lot of church's culture is the same way; the kitchen represents the staff, paid or volunteered, and the dining room represents the sanctuary. So, if there is fog in the back room (Kitchen), then there's going to be a lot of mist in the pews (Dining room). This means the congregational members have so much mist in their eyes that the vision will not be clear and their ears are dull of hearing correctly because the communication that is being spoken is not making any sense. So, the question is, how can we build a culture of evangelism that will be effective?

The military does air attacks to weaken the enemy, so they can send in the ground troops to finish it out, but in the body of Christ, Evangelism is not done just by the pastor pushing out air attacks that will weaken the congregation, but ultimately Evangelism is done by the ground troops which is the members or partners of a congregation.

When you are creating a culture of effective evangelism, it needs to be built from the bottom up and not top down. Even though multiple evangelism messages that are spoken starts at the top, which is from the Pastors and leadership team, the foundation of the message starts at the bottom because, without the people doing the everyday work of engaging others throughout their community, city, and state it will not work. Building a culture of effective evangelism without a foundation is like putting a roof on a house, then the floor and then the siding, it will be difficult, why? Because there needs to be something that holds up the roof. When you start to create and build a culture of effective evangelism everyone should be as one mind and heart with a mind to evangelize. Why, because all the people will understand that the main assignment of the church is to not just "do" witnessing, but to "be" an effective witness. Look at the following scripture.

"But you shall receive power (ability, efficiency, and might) when the Holy Spirit has come upon you, and you shall be My witnesses in Jerusalem and all Judea and Samaria and to the ends (the very bounds) of the earth."

Acts 1:8 AMPC

It's not just about the programs that builds effective evangelism, its ultimately about the people whose life has been transformed and equipped by the power and word of God and are willing to "go" share the Gospel with others, only then will you see the results of your labor.

10 For God is not unjust so as to forget your work and the love which you have shown for His name in ministering to [the needs of] the saints (God's people), as you do."

Hebrews 6:10 AMP

Love and kindness will always connect people to Jesus. Remember, buildings don't evangelize because buildings don't move, but people do. When people are not moving, they become stagnant and will eventually go from movement to becoming a monument. It's vitally important as I stated earlier, building a culture of effective evangelism is not just built with programs and personalities, but effective programs are built with people that have a heart for evangelism. Creating and building a culture of effective evangelism is one of the most difficult things that a church can attempt. Why? Because evangelism goes against almost everything in our self-centered culture!

You can have great vision for your church to grow, but if you are not willing to change the old culture to prepare for growth it will not happen. Why? Because old culture will always affect a new vision. The scripture says that you cannot put new wine in old wine skin, because if you do, it will be hard and difficult for the old culture to contain what is new which makes it very difficult to accept the new vision.

> *"No one puts new wine into old wineskins; otherwise the [fermenting] wine will [expand and] burst the skins, and the wine is lost as well as the wineskins. But new wine must be put into new wineskins."*

MARK 2:22 AMP

Too many church members have become absolute consumers of the word, but not contributors of the word. For over thirty years, I have been sharing with born again believers that "Jesus came to comfort the afflicted and to afflict the comfortable".

Jesus was very clear when He said, that if someone leaves a local church and you have not seen them in a while, what should you do? Because of the evangelism culture of your church, you should leave the others that are still attending and go after the one that has left.

"Look at it this way. If someone has a hundred sheep and one of them wanders off, doesn't he leave the ninety-nine and go after the one? And if he finds it, doesn't he make far more over it than over the ninety-nine who stay put? Your Father in heaven feels the same way. He doesn't want to lose even one of these simple believers."

Matthew 18:12-14 MSG

One of the major problems with churches across America is that the ninety-nine only care about the one, themselves. The most selfless thing a church can do is go and reach not just the lost, but the believer that is wandering as well. To create, build and grow a culture of effective evangelism. Dr. Ray Hampton says, "people need to get up out of their seat, on their feet and get in the streets and start sharing the gospel". One of the ways to do this is, the people that are in positions and power have to begin to equip and empower the congregation for evangelism, to start making room for the new and returning people who are getting ready to start attending the service. There are at least five things that you should do when creating and building a culture of evangelism.

FIVE KEY POINTS TO CREATE AND BUILD A CULTURE OF EVANGELISM

1. **BE AN EXAMPLE**

   You cannot expect people to do something that you will not do yourself.

2. **TEACH AND PREACH RELEVANT EVANGELISM MESSAGES**

A lot of churches desire to grow, but will not be committed to preaching relevant evangelistic messages or develop discipleship classes that will equip and empower the people in the congregation to invite their friends, neighbors, family members, and co-workers to church. Remember, "consistency is the key to church growth".

3. **CREATE AN ATMOSPHERE WHERE NON-BELIEVERS FEEL WELCOME**

As an evangelist, pastor, or teacher, if you are always preaching or teaching in a way that assumes everyone is a Christian, then people who aren't Christians will never be able to experience a transformed life. However, if you regularly address those in the room who are not Christians or right on the edge of becoming one, you accomplish two things: Number one, you are letting them know that they are welcome at the church and you are also creating an atmosphere where people can feel comfortable inviting their non-Christian friends, neighbors, family members, and co-workers because they know you will speak to them too. People will not invite other people to the church if they don't think it is a safe place for their guest. If they are worried that their non-Christian friends, neighbors, family members, and co-workers coming to church for the first time and hear a message preach or taught that has no relevancy to their lives whatsoever, they simply won't invite them.

However, if they know that you will address their non-Christian friends, neighbors, family members, and co-worker's life circumstances every single week, the fear of them inviting people and bringing them to church will be cancelled.

4. **HAVE A "WOW" FACTOR FOR PEOPLE TO INVITE OTHERS TO CHURCH**

In the business world, the "WOW" factor is a commonly used slang term in business that depicts what a company does to go above and beyond a customer's expectations in delivering a great product and service experience. Most often, it relates to exceptional customer service in which an employee gives the customer more than they expected or something they did not expect at all. What would happen if this same definition of the "WOW" factor happened in your local church or ministry? When people show up to your weekly services, they would receive more than what they expected or were told from the time they entered the premises to the time they exit the premises. Now, that's what I call moving up from coach to first class. All because of the first-class customer service they received from the parking lot attendants, greeters, ushers, musicians, singers, pastors, deacons, administrators, ministers, partners, members, custodians and etc. Now, that's graduating from being a consumer to a contributor. You must give the people who are currently attending your service something to be excited for and once they are excited it will give them a great excuse to invite others to come share in the excitement as well. I would like to call this "contact evangelism". Think about a sale you saw at a department store that was incredibly great, what did you do? You went and told somebody else about the great deals you saw and purchases you made. When Jesus met the woman at the well, what did she do after the conversation she had with Jesus? She was so excited that she went and told others and in response multiple people received Jesus because of her excitement.

"Then the woman left her water jar and went into the city and began telling the people, "Come, see a man who told me all the things that I have done! Can this be the Christ (the Messiah, the Anointed)?" So, the people left the city and were coming to Him. Now many Samaritans from that city believed in Him and trusted Him [as Savior] because of what the woman said when she testified, "He told me all the things that I have done.""

JOHN 4:28-30, 39 AMP

W.O.W. FACTOR

There are multiple ways through which you can create W.O.W. factors at your church. One of the simplest, but effective ways to create and build W.O.W. factor is to use the important holidays which, I like to call C.M.E. holidays. You're probably wondering what C.M.E. holidays. C.M.E. holidays are people that only come to church on **C**hristmas, **M**others' Day, and **E**aster. These people are going to attend anyway, so you might as well capitalize on the momentum. Other W.O.W. factor days are Father's Day, the weekend preceding fourth of July and the weekend preceding Thanksgiving. Whatever you do, circle a day or days on your calendar, promote and share with the people, that you want them to invite people on W.O.W. factor days.

Always remember, that "goals without dates are dreams". It sounds simple, but again, many churches will not be consistent in doing W.O.W. factor days or don't know how to create a W.O.W. factor day. That's why I have written this evangelism course, because I really believe that people know what they are called to do and even know why they are called to do it, but I believe the major issue is that many leaders and congregation members just don't know how to connect the what and the why.

Clearly tell people that you want them to invite people to these "WOW" factor events. Give them simple tools like invitation cards to hand out. You will be surprised how effective it is.

5. **CELEBRATE EVANGELISM**

When someone comes to your church and gives their life to Christ, celebrate it! When people get baptized, celebrate it! When someone in your church invites someone, celebrate it! When you hear about spiritual conversations that your people are having with friends or co-workers, celebrate it! When attendance is up, celebrate it!

Whatever gets celebrated in your church will get repeated. Celebrating evangelism shows everyone that this is what your church values. If the angels in Heaven celebrate whenever a lost person is found, it might be a good idea if we did too.

Make a big deal about it, why? Because it is a big deal! Creating and building a culture to have an evangelistically focused church starts with you. If you model evangelism, preach evangelism, create evangelistic environments, promote evangelistic opportunities, and celebrate evangelism, the people in the church will naturally become empowered for evangelism.

If you are already creating and building a culture of evangelism in your church, keep up the great work.

Continue to create, build, engage, equip, and empower people for a culture of evangelism.

I'm absolutely convinced that an evangelism culture is more effective than having an evangelism program.

In a church with a program driven approach to evangelism, sharing the gospel can become something mostly for certain people at certain times, like when the evangelism team goes out visiting. But in a church where there is creating, building, engaging, equipping, and empowering people for evangelism, the people are more encouraged to go out and evangelize, why? Because a culture is being created and it has now become a part of every born-again believer's life.

HOW TO CREATE AND BUILD A CULTURE OF EVANGELISM

1. **PRAYER**

A church that is sharing the gospel must be committed to prayer. An evangelistic culture church must have a foundation of prayer, to effectively create and build an evangelism culture. If people are nervous about sharing the gospel, encourage them to begin with prayer. They can pray that the Lord will give them opportunities to witness, and that He would direct individuals to them that need to hear the Gospel.

2. **GOSPEL MESSAGE**

A relevant gospel message is very important in creating and building an evangelistic church culture. The goal is to create an effective culture of evangelism not a program. To some people evangelism comes naturally, but to many people they need to be equipped to share the gospel. Have you ever thought about people who don't go to church and might not want to go to church? The real question is why don't people want to go to church? Maybe one of the reasons is because people don't want to be looked at as a number, but as an individual who is trying to have a relationship with Jesus. Whenever you put church attendance ahead of someone that is seeking to have a relationship with Jesus, you are sending people the wrong message that salvation is about church attendance and not about Jesus. I do realize that the following scripture says,

"Not forsaking or neglecting to assemble together [as believers], as is the habit of some people, but admonishing (warning, urging, and encouraging) one another, and all the more faithfully as you see the day approaching."

Hebrews 10:25 AMPC

Many leaders are more concerned about getting people to come to church, more than they are getting them to come to Jesus. When people are more committed to the church than they are to Jesus they will do some of the following:

- Attend weekly services, but not involved in too many or no ministries.
- Involved in every church activity possible, but neglecting things in their own marriage, family or even life.
- But when they are more connected to Jesus more than Church, they will do the following:
- Attend weekly services and get involved in their local church ministry, but not too many, so it doesn't neglect valuable time within their marriage, family, or daily life.
- Volunteer their labor of love for other non-profit ministries throughout their community, city, and state.
- Volunteer their finances to other worthy causes throughout their community, city, and state.

As a born-again believer in Christ your assignment as the set person is to introduce Jesus to people, more than church. Even though there is a connection, I rather introduce people to Jesus first because then they will want to fellowship with other believers.

I'm not saying to not talk about church or to not invite people to church, but the point I'm trying to get across is, "let's connect people to Jesus, so they will want to stay connected to church"

"Church attendance is not the goal. It's a tool to help us reach the goal"

One of the hardest things to do as an invitee when attending a local church is; Going to a new church and the second hardest thing for them to do is going to a new church where you're not already friends with someone who goes there.

This is even true with people who have been in a certain church for years and now it's time for a new assignment in their life to attend another church. It's very possible for even this individual to have a fear of the unknown and it's even worse when they have arrived at their new church, and no one greets or fellowships with them. As months or even years go by, genuine relationships were never built. Not because they weren't friendly, but because of a lack of genuine acceptance by others that were all already planted in that church. Inviting people to church is easy for the inviter, but can be very hard for the invitee. You might disagree with what I'm saying, but let me flip it and say it this way. Inviting them to your home is harder for you, but easier for them (Invitee).

"Jesus never made it hard for anyone to receive Him", I believe we should follow His example.

"It's great to go to a church that's friendly, but it's even better to go to church with a friend".

Chapter 3

INVITING SOMEONE TO CHURCH

The word **each** means everyone individually or one by one. To **reach** is to stretch or extend as to touch or to meet. Another definition would be to succeed in contacting, influencing, impressing, interesting or convincing. When looking at the word **one;** it means to be considered as a single unit or individually.

"Again, the next day, John stood with two of his disciples. And looking at Jesus as He walked, he said, "Behold the Lamb of God!" The two disciples heard him speak, and they followed Jesus. Then Jesus turned, and seeing them following, said to them, "What do you seek?" They said to Him, "Rabbi" (which is to say, when translated, Teacher), "where are You staying?" He said to them, "Come and see." They came and saw where He was staying and remained with Him that day (now it was about the tenth hour). One of the two who heard John speak, and followed Him, was Andrew, Simon Peter's brother. He first found his own brother Simon, and said to him, "We have found the Messiah" (which is translated, the Christ). And he brought him to Jesus. Now when Jesus looked at him, He said, "You are Simon the son of Jonah. You shall be called Cephas" (which is translated, A Stone). The following day Jesus wanted to go to Galilee, and He found Philip and said to him, "Follow Me." Now Philip was from Bethsaida, the city of Andrew and Peter. Philip found Nathanael and said to him, "We have found Him of whom Moses in the law, and also the prophets, wrote—Jesus of Nazareth, the son of Joseph." And Nathanael said to him, "Can anything good come out of Nazareth?" Philip said to him, "Come and see.""

⊙ Jesus called John and John followed Jesus

⊙ John reached Andrew and Andrew Followed Jesus

⊙ Andrew reached Peter and Peter followed Jesus

⊙ Jesus called Phillip and Phillip followed Jesus

⊙ Phillip reached Nathanael and Nathanael followed Jesus.

EACH of the disciples were reached **ONE** by **ONE**! And from **EACH** one **REACHING** one, the word of God was preached throughout the land and the gospel message went around the world. **EACH ONE** of them continued to **REACH ONE**, but it started with " **ONE REACHING ONE**"! _Once a person comes in contact with Jesus their life will immediately be impacted!_

{15} Now when one of those who sat at the table with Him heard these things, he said to Him, "Blessed is he who shall eat bread in the kingdom of God!" {16} Then He said to him, "A certain man gave a great supper and invited many, {17} and sent his servant at supper time to say to those who were invited, 'Come, for all things are now ready.' {18} But they all with one accord began to make excuses. The first said to him, 'I have bought a piece of ground, and I must go and see it. I ask you to have me excused.' {19} And another said, 'I have bought five yoke of oxen, and I am going to test them. I ask you to have me excused.' {20} Still another said, 'I have married a wife, and therefore I cannot come.' {21} So that servant came and reported these things to his master. Then the master of the house, being angry, said to his servant, 'Go out quickly into the streets and lanes of the city, and bring in here the poor and the maimed and the lame and the blind.' {22} And the servant said, 'Master, it is done as you *commanded, and still there is room.' 23 Then the master said to the servant, 'Go out into the highways and hedges, and compel them to come in, that my house may be filled. 24 For I say to you that none of those men who were invited shall taste my supper.'"*

Luke 14:15-24 NKJV

Every born-again believer should be part of a church that participates in sharing at least two things; Number one is inviting people to know Jesus and inviting them to a community of believers, which is the local church. Inviting people to a church doesn't happen automatically; it has to be a strategic and intentional effort. There needs to be a cultivating culture of inviting others to the church you attend.

For a lot of believers, it's a lot easier to welcome people to church once they have arrived, rather than going throughout the community or city to invite them to church. I believe that majority of Christians that attend church consistently know at least two things; the what and the why, but lack the knowledge of the how, they just don't know how to do it. So, I'm going to give you the following three steps to get you started on the Journey of inviting others to church, so we all can see and experience local community church growth and kingdom growth of believers that are not just Christians, but ultimately disciples, which are; followers of Jesus.

S.T.E.P.S. (Short Term Evangelism Process Strategy)

STEP # 1

The first step is to create a **culture of evangelism** in the church to invite people! It's so easy to get caught up in the regular rhythm of Sunday services and forget to ask the members or attenders to invite others to church at the next mid-week and or Sunday service. Yes, it's important for the announcements at the end of service, but don't be so quick to dismiss people because they have been in service for over two hours. I have been in multiple services where the announcements have been said or shown on the projector screen and there wasn't even an altar call extended to the people for salvation and no one was encouraged to invite someone to service the following week.

STEP #2

After you have created a culture of evangelism; now it's time to **equip the members** and attenders. It's important to offer verbal support and encouragement along with the tools that will assist them on the journey of inviting people to church. Invite cards are not the only way to equip the congregation every week, but it's a great equipping engagement tool for everyone to have. An invite card is one great idea because it contains all the basic information a potential guest needs to know to locate your church and visit. You can make them as small as a business card, or what I recommend is a two by four-inch glossy firm card just in case you want to include extra information. Also, it's vitally important to always keep a stack of cards on the table in the foyer or a place in the church where the cards are visible and accessible, so people will be able to pick up as needed. Don't forget to let the congregation know that the cards are available and highly encourage them to pick some up as well and prayerfully think of who they could offer one to. If they need to build their faith to invite someone, they can always leave a couple of cards at their place of work or a local business. I will be showing you the invite strategy later in this chapter.

STEP #3

A **personal engagement invitation** is another way to invite someone to church because there's an existing connection with the invitor and invitee. People will typically feel much more comfortable attending a new church when they already know someone there. It can help take away the anxiety of having to navigate around on their own, or the fear of sitting by themselves. Plus, when they visit church because of a personal engagement invitation from someone they know, they already have a point person to answer any questions they may have.

Now that you've explained to your church why inviting someone is important, make sure you're ready for a new guest! Your church members will feel a-lot more comfortable inviting people to church if they know their guests will arrive to a warm welcoming environment. If you haven't reviewed your guest services policies lately, this is a great time to review them before you read any further. Make sure your welcome desk is easily an accessible place that the new or returning guest can go to get all questions answered if needed. Your welcome desk volunteers should be very hospitable and well versed in virtually everything about how to get people more connected to the church. It's very important to have quarterly training for your welcome team, so that everyone can be consistent when giving out information, especially if you're periodically adding new volunteers to the team. Also, make sure the welcome desk is stocked with the items someone might need during the service, such as, but not limited to, bottled water, Kleenex, breath mints, pens, notepads etc.

A welcome gift bag or special items is also a great tool to hand out to your guest once they arrive, items such as; T-shirts, water bottles, coffee mugs, gift cards to local business etc. Now that you're all prepared for the new guest, how will you welcome them and show that they are valuable VIP's (Very

Important People)? Since they have already had a first-class welcome by the greeters and members of the church; the next thing is to acknowledge the guest at the beginning of the service. This will send a positive message to let them know that not only the welcoming team and other congregational members appreciate their presence, but the pastor and the staff does as well. It's been said over the years that "People don't care how much you know, but how much you care." It's not necessary to have the guest stand up or raise their hands. Why? Because some people are comfortable with standing up and raising their hands, but it could potentially be embarrassing for others. If you stay with the following verbiage, such as, "If you're a guest today, welcome! We're so glad that you are here." This is enough to make them feel like a valuable VIP (Very Important Person). Remember, if you do have guest stand up or raise their hand, at least hand them a gift, such as, but not limited to; a message of a sermon, note pad, pen, connection card, church information etc. If you're not going to hand them anything or allow them to speak, then why ask them to stand up or raise their hand.

When looking at our foundation scriptures in Luke chapter fourteen verses fifteen to twenty-four, there are three key focus words that jumps out of the scripture to me which are: *inviting, bringing, and compelling.*

- The word **invite** means: <u>To make a polite, formal or friendly request to someone to go somewhere or to do something.</u>

- The word **bring** means: <u>To arrive at the destination with someone.</u>

- The word **compel** means: <u>To force someone to do something</u>

In the text where Jesus stated the kingdom of God, He is referring to the future messianic banquet, where only Godly Jews would be invited. But Jesus uses this parable to let His listeners know that contrary to their expectations, that the original guests that were invited will miss the banquet and will be replaced by people that are poor, cripple, blind, lame and gentiles who were outsiders in the highways and hedges.

The streets and lanes within the city were the places where the Israelites who were considered the outcast lived, they were the poor, cripple, blind and lame. The highways and hedges which were on the outside of the city is where the gentiles lived. It was the custom to give advance notice by sending out invitations to a dinner. There were two invitations that would have been given out, the first one was an advance notice for the banquet. The second was a personal invitation that was handed out on the day of the banquet to let everyone know that today is the day, for the banquet is ready. Even though the guests that were invited had been given advance notices for the banquet they made excuses because they could not attend. The actions of their excuses show that they were putting their everyday life agendas before God. The first one let his possessions keep him away, the second one let his business keep him away, and the third one let his natural affections keep him away .God's invitation is for salvation and you can only get into His banquet by receiving a gift, the only thing that will exclude you from this banquet is the refusal to accept His invitation. You will not be able to buy your way into this banquet; the only way in is through the "grace of God".

8 For by grace you have been saved through faith, and that not of yourselves; it is the gift of God, 9 not of works, lest anyone should boast.

Ephesians 2:8-9 NKJV

1. If I showed you how you can have effective weekly, monthly, quarterly, and annual evangelism strategies and outreaches that could cause growth in your weekly attendance, would you be interested?

2. If I showed you how you can invite people to your church, would you be interested?

3. If I showed you how you can create a follow up system at your church to see people come back, would you be interested?

When inviting people to church, many believers know **what** they want to do, **why** they want to do it, but very few people know **how** to do it. My goal is to show you how to connect the what and why with the how, so you can receive effective results.

WHAT IS AN INVITATION?

For many of the unchurched, it's a *verbal invitation* to come to church. For others, it was an **invitation** to meet someone at church to show them around or walk them into the building. In either case, the process is simple. *If we invite them, they will come.*

The culture of low weekly church attendance can be explained by a lack of church members inviting others to church. As I travel across the country to preach and teach evangelism and outreach strategies, one of my main quotes is "Whatever you do throughout the week when it pertains to evangelism and outreach, will determine what happens on Sunday morning. Within one week there is one-hundred and sixty-eight hours given to everyone, and how you spend those hours inviting people to church will possibly manifest the following weekly service."

I've been asked the following question by thousands of people multiple times? "How much time should I give to evangelism and outreach?" My answers are always the same, your life should be an evangelism and outreach. The real question is, how much time?

- ⊙ 31,536,000 seconds a year
- ⊙ 31,622,400 seconds in a leap year
- ⊙ 525,600 minutes in a year
- ⊙ 527,040 minutes in a leap year
- ⊙ 8,760 hours in a year
- ⊙ 8,784 hours in a leap year
- ⊙ 365 days in a year
- ⊙ 366 days in a leap year
- ⊙ 52 weeks in a year

IDENTIFY

The first step to **inviting** someone to the church is to **identify** people who would be open to attending church.

There are a lot of people who identifies their self as a follower of Jesus, but are not consistent when it comes to attending a local church. The following scripture shows you how important it is for believers in Christ to meet.

> *"Not forsaking our meeting together [as believers for worship and instruction], as is the habit of some, but encouraging one another; and all the more [faithfully] as you see the day [of Christ's return] approaching."*
> **Hebrews 10:25 AMP**

Six groups of people to invite to church

FAMILY

The easiest people to approach and **invite** to church are your *family* members, such as uncles, aunts, nieces, nephews, and cousins. Why? Because these individuals know and trust you and may be open to joining you on Sunday's and mid-week services.

CLOSE FRIENDS

Close friends are also great way to **invite** people to church. Because you already have a close relationship and trust that they can help you **invite** others.

NEIGHBORS

Neighbors may be ideal people to **invite** to church. They live in close proximity to you, which means they probably live-in close proximity to your place of worship.

CO-WORKERS

The next group of people to approach with an **invitation** to church are your *Co-Workers* which is a big jump from family, friends, and neighbors. These individuals may not know you very well, which means you may have to work harder to gain their trust and recognize their needs for faith and community.

STRANGERS

Strangers will be very difficult to **invite** to church. Why? Because these individuals do not know you or have any kind of relationship with you. You may assume someone you meet needs faith or a spiritual community, but it can be hard to appeal to that person's needs if they don't already know you on some level. Remember, anyone can be invited to church, but the people who are closest to you will be easier to reach out to because they know you.

UNBELIEVERS

The easiest *unbelievers* to **invite** to church are those who have undergone a significant recent life experience. Relationship, religion, and faith brings people comfort during life events, especially in a season of any kind of loss or change of life. Some life events that may offer an opportunity to invite someone to church include:

- ⊙ The death of a loved one
- ⊙ A recent relocation/change of residency
- ⊙ A new job or school
- ⊙ A recent marriage
- ⊙ The recent birth of a child
- ⊙ A recent divorce
- ⊙ Family problems

⊙ A major illness (either for the individual themselves or someone they know)

Before you approach someone about attending church, you may want to consider when would be an ideal time to invite them. Having a firm date in mind will make it easier to **invite** someone, instead of a general open invitation. You can name a specific date and ask them is their schedule open for that day to be your guest at church.

Keep in mind that many people prefer to attend a church service on a Sunday, why? Because weekdays may be difficult because of work, traffic, school events, children practicing sports etc.… whereas Sundays are often a leisure day for most people who are working Monday through Friday.

Prayer is the foundational key for guidance when inviting someone to church. As you pray, ask for God's help for divine appointments to identify the right people, as well as the appropriate time to **invite** them to church. Any social event could be an opportunity to invite a person to church, who might be looking for a good church. If you spend a lot of time volunteering in your community or city, consider inviting people you meet at the events.

Once you've identified someone who would be open to attending church and chosen a specific date, you can now offer them an invitation to come with you to church. You should be courteous and respectful, even if the person declines your invitation. It may just be the wrong time, and that individual may be open to joining you in the future, if you show a little patience. Remember what the following scripture says.

"I planted the seed in your hearts, and Apollos watered it, but it was God who made it grow."

1 Corinthians 3:6 NLT

If the individual you've asked agrees to attend church with you, then you've obviously approached the right person at the right time. Go with them to church services and introduce them to as many people as you can, so they will feel welcome.

WHAT HAPPENS IF THE INVITEE SAYS "NO"

If the individual says no, that's okay too. You still have an obligation as a person of faith to show that individual love, kindness, and respect.

Collect your thoughts before you respond to a "no." Put yourself in the other person's shoes. Perhaps it's just not the right time for that individual, or perhaps they had a negative experience at another church in the past. Either way, it is not a reflection on you or your abilities.

Try to keep your emotions in check. Don't get upset if a person rejects your offer. Remember, according to the word of God, as a believer in Christ your assignment is to **invite, bring** and **compel** people to come to church, so they will become disciples of Christ.

Extend an open invitation, even if the person says no. You can say something respectful and **inviting**, such as "That's okay, I respect your decision. Just know that if you ever change your mind, my invitation always stands."

INVITING PEOPLE THAT YOU ARE NOT REALLY SURE ATTEND CHURCH

When you're not sure if a person attends a church.

Ask the following question:

I was wondering, do you go to church anywhere?

If they answer yes, then the follow-up conversation is easy.

That's great! So happy to hear you have a home church. What church do you attend?

This approach works because it celebrates the church they're connected to and shows them you're not trying to recruit them to your church.

If they answer no, you can follow up with an **invite**.

Well, if you're ever looking for a great place to go, I go to (insert your church name here) and would love to see you there!

This type of language will show that you are passionate and friendly. It doesn't assume they're looking for a church and leaves the decision up to them.

If they don't ask a follow-up question or engage further, then you'll want to stop the conversation regarding an invitation to church and bring up another friendly topic such as sports. If they ask a question or share a bit of their faith journey, then it's a good sign they're open to hearing more.

Take the opportunity to share more about your church and give them an **invite** card.

INVITING PEOPLE WHO DO NOT ATTEND CHURCH

When you know someone doesn't attend a church. Ask this question:

I'm curious, did you ever go to church when you were growing up?

The key that unlocks this question is how you follow up.

This question is an easy way to start a conversation, but the real value is learning more about a person's background with church, faith, and Christianity.

There could be many reasons why someone doesn't currently attend a church. They could've had a bad experience growing up. Been hurt by people. Maybe they've always wanted to go to church, but never made it a priority.

Whatever the reason, you're trying to understand why, so don't be afraid to ask the following follow-up questions.

- ⊙ Have you ever thought about attending church?
- ⊙ (If the answer is "NO" ask the following question)
- ⊙ If you don't mind me asking, how come you don't see yourself going to church?
- ⊙ If it's not too personal a question, what was the bad experience you had?

The answers to these questions will help you respond with a more personal invite at the right time. Use what you learn and ask God for wisdom on how best to **invite** them to church. That could be during this conversation or another time.

Is there something about your church they'd like? Is there a specific message series you can share that speaks to a situation they're going through? Do you apologize on behalf of other Christians or churches that have hurt them?

Remember, you don't have to **invite** a person the very first time you talk about church. That can be something you work toward. ***Building a relationship is always better than building religion.***

How do I avoid making a person feel judged or uncomfortable?

Pay attention to the conversation and engage as much or as little as you feel the other person is comfortable with. Follow the following six principles:

1. Be silent
2. Be a good listener
3. Remember main things within the conversation
4. Understand what they are saying
5. Don't Judge them
6. Make sure your action of response is sincere

The preceding six principles are how to **invite** someone or have a conversation about church, without the person feeling judged or uncomfortable.

How you end the conversation will be how they remember your **invite**. So, be kind, gracious, and understanding no matter the response.

WHAT HAPPENS IF I GET REJECTED?

You will, but don't let it discourage you. It's not the end of the world, and it's not personal.

A "no thanks" won't negatively impact your life. But a "yes" could change someone's life forever. Press through any fears of rejection and keep **inviting**! *__You'll never get a "yes"__* *__if you never ask.__*

Another common fear is getting a negative reaction, but almost everyone will accept your invite whether they're interested or not. As you invite more people, you'll find most of your fears are not reality. Rejection isn't as bad as you think. People generally avoid confrontation. They're not going to be hateful toward you or feel judged by you. God wants to use you and often, it's through a simple **invite**. If we do our part, God will do His part. We just have to plant the seed.

"Who do you think Paul is, anyway? Or Apollos, for that matter? Servants, both of us—servants who waited on you as you gradually learned to entrust your lives to our mutual Master. We each carried out our servant assignment. I planted the seed, Apollos watered the plants, but God made you grow. It's not the one who plants or the one who waters who is at the center of this process, but God who makes things grow. Planting and watering are menial servant jobs at minimum wages. What makes them worth doing is the God we are serving. You happen to be God's field in which we are working. Or, to put it another way, you are God's house. Using the gift God gave me as a good architect, I designed blueprints; Apollos is putting up the walls. Let each carpenter who comes on the job take care to build on the foundation! Remember, there is only one foundation, the one already laid: Jesus Christ. Take particular care in picking out your building materials. Eventually there is going to be an inspection. If you use cheap or inferior materials, you'll be found out. The inspection will be thorough and rigorous. You won't get by with a thing. If your work passes inspection, fine; if it doesn't, your part of the building will be torn out and started over. But you won't be torn out; you'll survive—but just barely."

1 Corinthians 3:5-9 MSG

54

Inviting a person to church is not the same thing as **inviting** them to know Jesus; **inviting** them to church is to be part of a community where they will meet Jesus.

"Improve the **process** you will improve the **results**"

THE REACH CYCLE
90 DAY EVANGELISM SOUL WINNING GROWTH FORMULA

Can be repeated for ultimate success

> *"The fruit of the [consistently] righteous is a tree of life, And he who is wise captures and wins souls [for God—he gathers them for eternity]."*

PROVERBS 11:30 AMP

1. The first **30 days** is all about making the culture or what you do a **HABIT**

   What is a HABIT? A HABIT is "an automatic reaction to a specific situation"

2. The next **30 days** is all about **CONSISTENCY**

   "Consistency is the key to church growth"

3. The last **30 days** is all about creating a **LIFESTYLE**

   "Goals without dates are just dreams"

> *"Now when one of those who sat at the table with Him heard these things, he said to Him, "Blessed is he who shall eat bread in the kingdom of God!" Then He said to him, "A certain man gave a great supper and invited many, and sent his servant at supper time to say to those who were invited, 'Come, for all things are now ready.' But they all with one accord began to make excuses. The first said to him, 'I have bought a piece of*

ground, and I must go and see it. I ask you to have me excused.' And another said, 'I have bought five yoke of oxen, and I am going to test them. I ask you to have me excused.' Still another said, 'I have married a wife, and therefore I cannot come.' So that servant came and reported these things to his master. Then the master of the house, being angry, said to his servant, 'Go out quickly into the streets and lanes of the city, and bring in here the poor and the maimed and the lame and the blind.' And the servant said, 'Master, it is done as you commanded, and still there is room.' Then the master said to the servant, 'Go out into the highways and hedges, and compel them to come in, that my house may be filled. For I say to you that none of those men who were invited shall taste my supper.' ""

Luke 14:15-24 NKJV

Three different ways were given out throughout the preceding scriptures to have people attend church:

1. **INVITED** = *Was the Unselected Group*
2. **BRING** = *Was a selected group*
3. **COMPEL** = *Others*

   "WHEN INVITING SOMEONE TO CHURCH YOU'RE NOT INVITING THEM TO A BUILDING, YOU ARE INVITING THEM TO HAVE A CONVERSATION WITH YOU THAT WILL BUILD A RELATIONSHIP TO INVITE THEM TO CHURCH *"REMEMBER YOU ARE THE CHURCH"*

"Welcome with open arms fellow believers who don't see things the way you do. And don't jump all over them every time they do or say something you don't agree with—even when it seems that they are strong on opinions but weak in the faith department. Remember, they have their own history to deal with. Treat them gently. For instance, a person who has been around for a while might well be convinced that he can eat anything on the table, while another, with a different background, might assume he should only be a vegetarian and eat accordingly. But since both are guests at Christ's table, wouldn't it be terribly rude if they fell to criticizing what

the other ate or didn't eat? God, after all, invited them both to the table.
Do you have any business crossing people off the guest list or interfering
with God's welcome? If there are corrections to be made or manners to be
learned, God can handle that without your help."

Romans 14:1-4 MSG

ONE...

INVITE 1

Each person receives **6** invite cards every week, to invite **6**
individuals to Church. The invite cards are strategically given
out to people, such as, but not limited to; people you come in
personal contact with every day.

Example: A congregation of **10** people can invite **60**
people a week that's **240** people a month that was invited
through contact evangelism from a church of **10** people. If only
1% of the people that were invited showed up every month
that's **2** new people added each month to a congregation of **10**
and in three months **6** new people which means, the
congregation has now grown to **16** new people in **90** days
almost doubling the congregation in size or **12** people in six
months or **24** people in one year.

NOW THATS INCREDIBLE!!!!!

It gets better......

TWO...

BRING 1

Each person brings **1** new person to church every week.

Example: A congregation of **10** people can bring **1** new person a week that's **10** people a week or **40** people a month that was brought to church by **1** person through contact evangelism from a church of **10** people.

If only **1%** of the new people became members of the church every month, that's **4** new people added to the congregation each month which is a total of **12** new people in three months doubling the congregation size in **90** days or **24** people in six months or **48** people in one year.

NOW THATS EVEN MORE INCREDIBLE!!!!!

It gets better......

THREE...

COMPEL 1

Each person compels **1** person a month to come to church. The word compel means; "to not listen to their excuses just bring them to church." **Example:** If a Church of **10** people compel **1** person <u>every two weeks (Twice a month)</u> and brought them to church. The monthly attendance can increase by **20** people a month.

If only **1%** of the new people became members of the church every month that's **2** new people added to the congregation each month which is a total of **6** new people in three months which is a total of **16** people; almost doubling the congregation in size in **90** days or **12** new people in six months or **24** people in one year.

If only **1%** show back up every week that was compelled to come twice a month by the church membership of **10** people, that's growth of **2** people every month or **24** people in one year

WOW!!!

ONE YEAR...........

As you continue this **1%** pace, look at the following amazing growth number totals of attenders/members within five years!!!

1% of the total of people that were **INVITED, BROUGHT** or **COMPEL** to church was **96** which means:

"ONE YEAR" the congregation of **10** is now a congregation of **106** people rising above the national church attendance size of a growth.

- ⊙ TWO YEARS....**202**
- ⊙ THREE YEARS....**298**
- ⊙ FOUR YEARS....**394**
- ⊙ FIVE YEARS....**490**

SIMPLE AS 1,2,3

WOW...THAT'S GREAT CHURCH GROWTH!!!

Remember,"1% of something is better than 0% of nothing". <u>THIS SYSTEM WILL WORK IF YOU WORK IT"</u>

Chapter 4

THE BEGINNING

1981-1990

It all started in 1981 at the age of sixteen years old. I was invited to stand in as the bass guitarist for a group call Gospel generation. We were invited to perform in the city Everett, WA. at a 3:00pm program at the Bible Way Church of God in Christ where Jerry Ramsey was the Pastor. As the service was in progress, I could not help noticing the young lady that was playing the piano. Perhaps it was the freckles on her face and the shiny curly hair that continued to shake as she directed a twenty plus youth choir from the piano. I probably can imagine what you might be thinking about right now. Why did I focus on the piano player rather than the church service? Well, that is an easy answer. I once was blind, but now I can see or shall I say, "The Lord is my Shephard and I see want I want". I think you understand what I mean, especially if you are a man. Anyway, I think I better continue with this story because if I do not it might not get finished, so let me continue. The close of the service could not come fast enough, because you already probably figured out by now, I had an agenda which was to get her phone number before I left the building. I was not thinking about an altar call for salvation or getting filled with the Holy Spirit or as the older saints would say, "feel him with the Holy Ghost'. If those mothers of the church, missionaries, elders, or deacons would have had me stay after for an altar call, I would have made sure to have one eye open to make sure that Julia did not leave out of the building. I did hear the preacher say earlier to "watch and pray", so I figured this was my opportunity to be obedient to do what the preacher said, watch and know were Julia was at all times as I was praying. The following scriptural text is what he quoted.

> *"Keep watch and pray, so that you will not give in to temptation. For the spirit is willing, but the body is weak!""*

Matthew 26:41 NLT

Now I know that I am doing more of an isagetical rather than a correct exegetical of the text. You might be wondering what the difference is. Well, there is a difference, the isagesis of the text is you trying to speak to the text, making it say what you want it to say. The exegesis of the text is allowing the word of God to speak to you. To break it down even more, you need to know the three C's; content, clarity, and conviction of the scriptural text. Well, as you can see by now, I was listening to the preacher, preach the word of God, but my mind was on Julia. According to the last part of the text, which is: "For the spirit is willing, but the body is weak!" So according to text perhaps, I probably was falling into temptation (Do not Judge Me). Once the altar was completed and the service was finish, I jumped up from that altar like popcorn popping in a pan of hot grease, or for the rest of you, like popcorn popping in bag in the microwave. Either way, I popped up with a quickness. Once I got up from the altar, I felt like 747-jet plane on a Boeing airport runway headed destination exit door to try to go get Julia's phone number. Well, it was not as easy as I had expected, because she did not give me her number, but thank God for a young niece that was willing to give out family numbers. PRAISE THE LORD! When I finally got a moment to call her that evening, of course you already know what I was going to ask, which was," Would she like to go out somewhere?". I know as you're reading this that you're probably thinking "where is somewhere?" When you're sixteen years old; somewhere is anywhere as long as I was able to get a date or shall I say take her out. After multiple days and weeks went by, she kept refusing to go any place with me. I will always remember the day when she finally said yes! And it was her birthday month as well. As you already know, because of my persistency of pursuing Julia, I felt like I was balling and in alignment with the scripture that says,

5 And He said to them, "Which of you shall have a friend, and go to him at midnight and say to him, 'Friend, lend me three loaves; 6 for a friend of mine has come to me on his journey, and I have nothing to set

before him'; 7 and he will answer from within and say, 'Do not trouble me; the door is now shut, and my children are with me in bed; I cannot rise and give to you'? 8 I say to you, though he will not rise and give to him because he is his friend, yet because of **his persistence** *he will rise and give him as many as he needs."*

Luke 11:5-13 NKJV

Our first date was at a Hong's restaurant in Lynnwood, next door to the Lynnwood Skate deck. The night started out great with some very tasteful Chinese food to celebrate her eighteenth birthday. It was such an amazing evening eating great food and a night to remember; it was full of fun and fellowship. It is amazing how you will activate your Faith when you really desire something, and I knew at that very moment God was getting ready to bless me with the desire of my heart.

4 "Delight yourself also in the LORD, And He shall give you the desires of your heart."

Psalms 37:4 NKJV

Now, I know what you're probably thinking about, how a 16-year-old knew what God's heart desire was for him. Well, this is my answer to you, God knows my heart and where you might look at the outer appearance. God was looking at my heart the whole time, as a matter of fact, He's always been better to me than I've been to myself. God knew deep on the inside what I desire for life, and He was delivering my future wife to me right to my hands. Well, guess what? I was believing for this relationship to have everlasting favor that will last forever and at the time of writing of this book, we have been like a first-class stamp on an envelope going through the Journies of life celebrating thirty-nine years of marriage and counting. One of my favorite songs growing up as a teenager was by a group known as Heatwave. Heatwave had produced a number one song titled, "Always and forever" which was a great slow jam (A slow romantic song). Well, let me stop right here because you will hear more about this song a little later as you continue to read. As February was closing out, June was fastly approaching and the next four months came quickly along with two promotions. The first one was that I was moving from being a Junior to a senior in High School and Julia was graduating from high school, which meant she was on her way to Pullman, Washington, the home of Washington State University. WOW! As you can imagine, the next two months were not going to be easy for me because I did not want her to leave. Can you imagine a young lady in college exposed to all those college men, but dating a young man that was still in high school? Well, at that moment I knew I needed a miracle and I Knew my God was a miracle worker. The day came for Julia to depart for Washington State University and guess what, I was saddened and even cried (Do not laugh or judge me). Not because she hurt me, but because I felt alone living on the west side of the mountains without my girlfriend. Well, the time had finally come for Julia to leave for the university, but I felt a song come up in my spirit that they would sing during praise service at Bible Way Church of God in Christ. The words were "I got a feeling that everything is going to be alright ". Oh, how the people of God would sing and shout and dance once they receive their revelation that "everything is going to be alright, no matter what they were going through". I just want to pause right here and say that "It's your level of expectation that is connected to your revelation" that will bring you great results! My level of expectation was big concerning my girlfriend, Julia. As the months passed by and halfway through my senior year, we continued to stay in contact, but something amazing happen. This High school student asked the university student to marry him. And guess what? She said YES! The shocker was that it was about a year to the date when we met. January 1981 is when we met at the church and January 1982 is when I asked Julia to marry me.

"Who so findeth a wife findeth a good thing, and obtaineth favour of the Lord."

Proverbs 18:22 KJV

I knew Julia was trustworthy and definitely a good-looking girl from the first time I laid eyes on her, so that meant, I was going to be riding with favor, eating with favor, enjoying life with favor, and even one day having a family with favor. I must admit that for over 39 years plus; the lord has put His stamp of approval on our marriage. Did you notice how the word favor is spelled out in this text? It's FAVOUR the difference is you got it right, it's the letter "U". Whenever God gives you favor, He always has you ("U") on His mind. That was my confirmation that my life with Julia was going to be great!

It is 1982 and the time has now come for my high school graduation, not only was I graduating, but I was also preparing to move into my own apartment and get married. My graduation was held on June tenth at the paramount theatre in Seattle, Washington and believe me, it was a night to remember as there were multiple family and friends that were in attendance. Wow! What an amazing graduation night it was. There were so many family members and friends in attendance at the paramount in downtown Seattle to see me graduate from Lynnwood high school. It was a great night full of fun and activities; many people over the thirty plus years have asked me, were you first in your class? And my response is always YES! Julia was a senior class speaker at Everett High School who had done extremely well in class assignments, sports and of course the greatest and best-looking cheerleader that has ever walked the halls of Everett High School. Okay enough about Julia or I'll never get this book done. Let's get back to my class rank in my 1982 graduation. Since you know a little bit about Julia's graduation, my status of first in my class was the same, but there was a difference. I want you to know that I was first in my class; you heard it here, first in my class even though it was at the bottom third of the class I was still number one, but I graduated (Nothing else needs to be said about this matter) and have the Diploma to prove. What's understood doesn't need to be discussed any further. GO ROYALS!

Six weeks later at the age of seventeen years old; I rented my first apartment at the green view Apartment Homes located in Mount Lake Terrace, Washington. Would you believe if I told you that the apartment, I rented was only $295 dollars a month and every room was furnished with brand new furniture. I guarantee you that if you try to go look for the same type of layout I had at the same price with brand new furniture in today's market, you'll probably get very discouraged because you won't find it. But on the other hand, if you're really sincere and willing to walk by faith and not by sight and if there is something that you really want to happen for your life, here's my advice to you, "do what you have to do, so you can do what you need to do". My finances were in order because upon graduation my parents had given me a portion of our family Janitorial service. The name of the Janitorial service was R and H janitorial service, you probably can figure out what the R and H stand for by now. When I was in the 8th grade, my father and mother stepped out on faith to provide for the family by starting a janitorial service and every morning before my brothers, sisters and I went to school; we will wake up at 1:00am at least three days a week to go clean buildings, such as; Military recruiting offices, bowling alleys, taverns, real estate offices and on some Saturdays. We would even clean homes for people that were too busy in their entrepreneur lifestyle. One thing for sure is we always made it back home in time to be ready for school and be at the school bus stop.

When I was younger; I didn't understand really what was going on, but as I got older my father was keeping all the money in the family to make sure that we had a great life.

I was able to make $795 every two weeks cleaning post offices. My parents had owned the R & H Janitorial service six years prior to me graduating and had built a very successful family business with multiple contracts throughout the Snohomish and King Counties in the state of Washington. As time went on, the contracts I was working ended, but God had us covered.

I was hired at Denny's Restaurant as a dish washer making $2.90 cents an hour and as time went on, I even received two raises, first one to $3.10 and then $3.40 an hour. As time went on, I decided to change jobs that even paid me more money, so I applied at Shari's restaurant in Woodinville, Washington making almost $4.00 an hour, then I hit the Jack pot. Are you ready to hear this? I received a job at Black Angus located on highway 99 in Everett, Washington washing dishes, but now I am paid $5.00 an hour. I was known throughout the restaurant industries as a master dish washer. Now, as you are reading this, a master dishwasher might not seem important to you, but at least l was known for something positive. What type of work are you known for?

> *"Don't you remember the rule we had when we lived with you? "If you don't work, you don't eat." And now we're getting reports that a bunch of lazy good-for-nothings are taking advantage of you. This must not be tolerated. We command them to get to work immediately—no excuses, no arguments—and earn their own keep. Friends, don't slack off in doing your duty."*

2 Thessalonians 3:10-13 MSG

I must admit to you that at the age of nineteen I absolutely love to eat and if I had to work to do it, working a Job would not be any problem at all. Just sign me up. Oh yeah, working also allowed me to take care of my family; I almost forgot to mention that part.

In the spring of 1984, the word was out that Washington State University was encouraging individuals and especially families who were interested in a higher education to send in an application to admissions to be considered for enrollment in the school. After hearing this multiple times I decided to contact Aaron Haskins who was a recruiter for the Washington State University. After completing and turning in the required paperwork, my wife and I received great news! We were both admitted to the university; this was my first time, but for my wife she was returning (two years later) after completing her freshman year, but this time she was married with our first child, Trenecsia who was two years old. It was great to be going to the University as a family because it meant no dormitory living, but family Housing.

Well, it is time for new beginnings. I'm now officially a student enrolled in a university. The graduation class of Lynnwood High School would be proud of me. I graduated at the top of my class (even though it was the bottom third of the class) no matter how you look at it was still at the top. Anyway, let us move on. It is time for me to pursue my passion which was to start the Journey of becoming a physical therapist.

It's the month of august and as the school year getting ready to start, there was excitement every where on campus!

There were many get together with families and friends. I was invited to a beginning of the year Barbeque at the Home of Aaron Haskins where there was so much cooked food. I thought I was at the Kings table, old Country buffet, Country harvest, Golden Corral, Ryan's or (Say the name of your favorite all you can eat buffet) as you can see basically, I thought I was at a all you can eat buffet! As the day went on, one of the students had entered the living room holding a big platter of barbecue ribs. Well, you already know what I was thinking, it's time to eat. After multiple great conversations with everyone, a supernatural friendship was growing with an individual name Charlie Hill, who was the one with the platter of ribs. I mean, we connected like a stamp on an envelope and the rest were history. We began to hang out and I mean, we hung out all the time and I literally mean, all the time. As our friendship continued to grow, one of our meetings was playing a lot of basketball at one of the campus gyms (everyday). Day after Day, I would hear the other in the gym between games talk about a place called JW's in Moscow Idaho. Moscow, Idaho was only eight miles away from Pullman and home of the university of Idaho. The minimum age in the state for night clubs that year was only nineteen years old for entry into, what was known as; the club instead of twenty-one. Throughout my freshman year, it was classes almost every day, basketball every other day and JW" s Friday and Saturday nights.

After my freshman year was completed and summer had ended, I was, like the scripture says,

""The harvest is past, the summer is ended, and we are not saved!"
Jeremiah 8:20 NKJV

As we returned to school for the second year; something amazing happened on a Friday night September 27, 1985. As I was getting dressed to go out with my friend, Charlie Hill, someone knocked on the door and when I answered, to my amazement, it was Charlie and his wife. I knew at that very moment (because he was with his wife) it was not going to be business as usual, which meant I had a feeling we would not be going out to JW's dance club. Charlie began to share with me how earlier in the day his wife Lisa and himself had prayed the prayer of salvation and he had rededicated his life to Jesus. I was shocked because it was a Friday night and for the first year at Washington State university, we always, and I mean always went to the dance club on Friday nights and sometimes even on a few Saturdays (okay most Saturdays). I was so excited for him, but I was also excited about going back out to the club until the next words came out of his mouth. He said, there was a revival on campus at the Compton Union Building (Known as the C.U.B.) and the speaker was an evangelist named Greg Ball, who was brought in by Maranatha Ministries. Then he asked me a question that would change my life forever. He invited me to attend the revival meeting with him. Within the hour, we were on our way to the revival. Upon our arrival, one of the Pastors of Maranatha Ministries whose name was Aaron Haskins noticed the both of us in the meeting and invited us to move to the front row. At that moment, my quick-thinking answer was no, I am fine. The truth is, I wanted to make sure that I had a quick exit to the door once the service was over because my intentions were still to make it to the club with or without Charlie. As the evangelist was bringing his sermon to a close, the last thing he offered was an altar call and by now you probably know what happened. Well, you are right, when the evangelist offered the call for salvation, I began to feel something all over me. The presence of the Holy Spirit was tugging, pulling and ministering to my spirit. When the evangelist said, "If you feel the presence of the Holy Spirit; raise your hand ". You can imagine what I was thinking and you're right, I was like "Oh no, what's going on and before I knew it, I had walked up to the front of the church to accept Jesus Christ into my life.

> *"Therefore, if anyone is in Christ [that is, grafted in, joined to Him by faith in Him as Savior], he is a new creature [reborn and renewed by the Holy Spirit]; the old things [the previous moral and spiritual condition] have passed away. Behold, new things have come [because spiritual awakening brings a new life]."*

2 Corinthians 5:17 AMP

When I returned home that evening and Charlie told my wife that I had some great news to share with her. As she began to smile along with myself, Charlie and Lisa, she was patiently waiting for the news. My wife was raised in the church all her life and she had known that when we left earlier, we were headed to the revival. Maybe she had an idea what might have happened, but it needed to come out of my mouth not hers. I guess, I was taking too long to say it partially because I kept smiling. Eventually Charlie said, come on Hambone say it. I had two nicknames while I was at W.S.U. Hambone was one and "Daddy Ray" was the other; both names created and given. Who do you think gave me those nicknames? You guess it right, my friend Charlie. Now since you know my nicknames, it be only right for me to say Charlie is also. Here it is CJ Wind Walker Jam Jr. so, now you know. Now, do not laugh at our nicknames, I'm sure you had or have one as well. The revival was on a Friday night and two days later I was in church singing, "Thank you Lord for all you've done for me". It was very important that I gave God all the praise for my life. The enemy thought he had me, but I escaped his hold and was no longer in bondage. As Martin Luther King said and I Quote "Free at last, Free at last, Thank God almighty we are Free at last" I was no longer a slave to sin, now I was righteous in God.

"You are of God, little children, and have overcome them, because He who is in you is greater than he who is in the world."

I John 4:4 NKJV

"Now we're no longer living like slaves under the law, but we enjoy being God's very own sons and daughters! And because we're his, we can access everything our Father has —for we are heirs because of what God has done!"

Galatians 4:7 TPT

"For God made Christ, who never sinned, to be the offering for our sin, so that we could be made right with God through Christ."

2 Corinthians 5:21 NLT

The next three years at the University was life changing. We started to attend the All

Nations Church Pastored by Roosevelt & Vicki Currie, where my spiritual growth started to excel. This might not be a big deal to you as you're reading this, but trust me, to live a life serving the Lord on a university campus as a twenty-year-old you have to be serious. The club scene was done, but the basketball playing was still in full effect.

In 1986, our family began to expand with our second child who was born on December 9, 1986 at Pullman Memorial. I remember the day well because we already had a daughter who was three years old and now, we were getting ready for our first son. Having a son was awesome because his name is, are you ready for this? His name is Raymond Hampton IV. Just in case you're wondering, my grandfather Raymond Hampton is Sr., dad is Jr., I'm the III and now there is an IV. It gets even better, now my grandson is the V and none of us have a middle name. To keep it even more interesting, our family names are as follows; Old man Raymond (Grandfather), Raymond (Dad), RayRay (Myself), Ramon (Son) and Rai (Grandson). I hope as you're reading this, you're saying to yourself; this is doing too much. Do not blame me, I didn't start this legacy; I'm just continuing the legacy. Hmmmm… I wonder what my grandson is going to do. Whether he does continue or not; it's the by the grace of

God we made it to number 5. Just in case you are wanting to see what's next!

After spending four years at Washington State University the time had come for us to move

back to the other side of the mountains. In 1988, we returned to our hometown of Everett, Washington. Once we arrived, we were able to find a new residence in Lake Stevens, Washington. My wife and I was expecting our third child. On August 4th, 1988, Michael James Hampton was born at the University Hospital in Seattle, Washington. Now, we had two sons, one was born in Pullman, Washington home of the Cougars and the other was born in Seattle Washington, home of the Huskies.

Upon our arrival, I immediately started to apply for employment at multiple job sites which eventually I was offered a Job at the Safeway distribution center in Bellevue, Washington where I was hired to work in the frozen food Warehouse. The starting wage was at $9.50 an hour and six months later, I received a raise to $11.50. My work assignment was working in a huge 30 below freezer. I rode a pallet jack up and down aisles picking orders that filled up the pallets then wrapped it up and wrote the store number on it, so it can be delivered to the correct store. Upon arrival, the night stockers can unwrap it and stock the product on the shelves, so customers can purchase the item. This is the first time that I had a Job starting at 4:00 am in the morning. To start a Job at 4:00am in the morning was not what I called the ideal work time for me to start a work, but I must admit I believed that God was teaching me how to trust and thank Him for everything.

> *"in every situation [no matter what the circumstances] be thankful and continually give thanks to God; for this is the will of God for you in Christ Jesus."*

1 Thessalonians 5:18 AMP

What kept me waking up morning after morning was that I knew that I was in the will of God, and He knows what is best for me. Whatever you're going through in life just remember one major thing, which is; you are being set up for something great, so stop whining, complaining, making excuses and know that you're in the will God for your life. Even sometimes you might not be able to trace Him (God), but you can always trust Him (God). Imagine how the three Hebrew boys who were thrown in the fiery furnace felt.

> *"And these three men, Shadrach, Meshach, and Abed-Nego, fell down bound into the midst of the burning fiery furnace. Then King Nebuchadnezzar was astonished; and he rose in haste and spoke, saying to his counselors, "Did we not cast three men bound into the midst of the fire?" They answered and said to the king, "True, O king." "Look!" he answered, "I see four men loose, walking in the midst of the fire; and they are not hurt, and the form of the fourth is like the Son of God.""*

Daniel 3:23-25 NKJV

You see, even when you can't trace Him (God) in every situation through life, all you really need to do is trust Him because He (God) was there all the time. I knew in my heart to do what I wanted to do, I needed to do what I had to do. Whatever passion, purpose and plan that has been outline for your life you will never arrive there if you keep trying to take short quick routes. When I'm cooking food for taste; I just don't want it seasoned well, I also want it to taste great! For this to happen, the food has to be cooked and seasoned the right way. One thing is for sure, food doesn't taste the same in a microwave as it does when it's prepared in an oven. How many times have you put a burrito or some other type of food in the microwave and the outside was done (not crisp), but the inside wasn't? One great thing about the oven is it will always cook food, not just on the outside but on the inside to perfection.

The lesson here is, be patient and not anxious, stop looking for a short cut.

"Do not be anxious or worried about anything, but in everything [every circumstance and situation] by prayer and petition with thanksgiving, continue to make your [specific] requests known to God."

Philippians 4:6 AMP

This reminds me of a song one of the Deacons or Mothers of the church would sing. Either at offering time or during testimony service. If you were raised in the church or attended a church with the following: Tambourine, drums, guitars, piano; for some of you it was an upright piano where you had to open the top lid or perhaps it could've been a fender Rhodes or a Hammond B-3 organ. I have a couple questions for you? At the church you attended, did they run around the pews/seats in the sanctuary? Was the hand clapping on the 2nd and 4th beat? Was there a loud "Thank You Jesus"? Was there shouting or what others might call dancing once the choir starts singing or was there ever an impromptu or spontaneous shout? I think by now you know what I mean when I say a testimony service. I don't know about you, but personally when I think about how great God has been to me, I have to take a pause for the cause and say, "Thank you Lord for all you've done for me". Since 2001, I've had the privilege of being a season ticket holder, receiving over 30 tickets a year, sitting in the End zone Known as the "Hawks Nest" for one of the greatest football teams in the world, the Seattle Seahawks. If you are thinking that the Seahawks are not a great team, my questions to you are; who is your favorite team? Do you support the team? That's what I thought. I recall going to a Seahawk game and during halftime decided to go to the concession stand to purchase a hot dog (okay I'll be honest, two dogs), garlic fries and a bottled water. Anyway, as I was headed back to my seat (Hawks Nest) I noticed that I had forgotten to put some Ketchup on the hotdogs and then something hit me. This is symbolic to a lot of people today, stop asking God to bless you today when truthfully you haven't thanked or given Him praise for what He has already done. Just in case you're wondering, what does all this have to do with forgetting the ketchup? Many people are always asking Jesus to bless them right now today and most of the time Jesus is saying you haven't thanked me for what I've already done yesterday, last week, last month or even last year, so you need to give Him a Ketchup (Catch up) praise!

After working for Safeway for about a year and half; the fourth-five-minute drive from Lake Stevens every morning was taking its toll. I eventually applied for a Job ten miles from my home at Hewlett & Packard as a wave solder operator and guess what? I got it, they hired me. It was a great job with benefits and flex time. Even though financially it provided for our needs, it still wasn't very fulfilling to the passion and purpose that I felt God had for me. The next Job I applied to work at was Bayliner Boat and Yacht lamination as a custodian. My job schedule was working the swing shift, which was from 3:00-11:30 pm, but this Job also wasn't very fulfilling to my passion and purpose, so I moved onto another Job trying to fulfill my passion and purpose. I started to work for Everett General Hospital as a dietary technician which was a position, I held for six months. After six months as a dietary technician, I then transferred departments to custodial services. Now, you're probably thinking or saying about now, 'Why did you keep changing jobs?' To be very honest with you, it wasn't the job, pay or the distance; it was about two major things; what was my "passion and purpose" for my life. I knew that God had a plan for my life and when I find out what it is, I was going to be all in. As I was looking into a mirror one day, I realized that God had made me an original not a copy, and that it was okay to be different. Whenever you look in the mirror, what do you see? I'm sure you see a mirror reflection of yourself, but I want you to know you're not just looking at a copy of yourself, you're looking at your original self. How? Because mirrors are made of glass and glass comes from sand and sand comes from the dust of the ground. When you were created, you were created from the dust of the earth, so therefore you were created to be an original not a copy of anyone else.

> *"Then the Lord God formed [that is, created the body of] man from the dust of the ground, and breathed into his nostrils the breath of life; and the man became a living being [an individual complete in body and spirit]."*

> **Genesis 2:7 AMP**

> *"All go to one place: all are from the dust, and all return to dust."*
> **Ecclesiastes 3:20 NKJV**

The black, red, and white that I read daily and meditate on helps me to stay focusED. Just in case you're wondering what the black, red, and white is, it's known as "The word of God" "The Bible". Oops... I forgot the other reason why I kept changing Jobs is because I like to eat so it was vitally important that 1 kept working seven days and twenty-four hours a day.

"Even while we were with you, we gave you this command: "Those unwilling to work will not get to eat.""

2 Thessalonians 3:10 NLT

During the year of 1990, my wife and I were expecting our fourth child. On February 10th at the Everett General Hospital in Everett, Washington, we were blessed with a gorgeous little girl, whose name is Catrena Sharde Hampton. During the pregnancy and after, I was also in my first year of semi-professional football playing for the Snohomish County Blue Nights where I had a very successful year on the defense of line as nose guard. Since I never received a phone call from any of the teams in the National Football League on draft day, I figured time was running out. If you're wondering what all this has to do with "Taking it to the streets". It has a lot to do with it because anything that stands firm forever was built on a solid foundation.

""These words I speak to you are not incidental additions to your life, homeowner improvements to your standard of living. They are foundational words, words to build a life on. If you work these words into your life, you are like a smart carpenter who built his house on solid rock. Rain poured down, the river flooded, a tornado hit—but nothing moved that house. It was fixed to the rock."

Matthew 7:24-25 MSG

For the last 30 years and counting, Ray Hampton Outreach Ministries has been built on a solid foundation and that "Rock is Jesus".

"And drank water from the same spiritual rock that traveled with them—and that Rock was Christ himself."

1 Corinthians 10:4 TPT

Chapter 5

TAKING IT TO THE STREETS

1991-1993

In the spring of 1991, I was offered a paid internship to work with the University of Washington football team as an athletic trainer making $795.00 a month under the guidance of Dennis Sealy. The following summer I enrolled into Seattle Pacific University athletic training program to start working with athletes who needed physical therapy, such as, but not limited to; ankle and knee wrap etc. I just knew if I could get more head knowledge of an athletic trainer, I would be one of the best trainers in sports.

During the month of July, I was listening to the local news station on channel 7 regarding the growing numbers of the homeless and hungry people that were living on the streets in downtown Everett. There began to be a stirring within myself to go do what I can to reach people that seem like everyone else had forgotten. If this was true or not, it did not matter to me. I knew that my response was my responsibility and that I couldn't change the world, but if I change my world everything around me had to change.

85

I started feeling very passionate about meeting the needs of people by "finding a need and fill it and a hurting hurt and heal it. I thought my passion and purpose was to become an athletic trainer, but it wasn't. My passion was to help people and I quickly realized that my purpose was not creating my passion, but my passion was creating my purpose for life. Even though I enjoyed being an athletic trainer working with people it was to get me to realize that there was even a greater calling on my life. There are all types of plans that you as an individual can have for your life, but I would like to challenge you by saying that your plans might not be your purpose for your life.

"Many plans are in a man's mind, But it is the LORD'S purpose for him that will stand (be carried out)."

Proverbs 19:21 AMP

Your strength will only come through your connection with God's purpose for your life not your plans; one of my favorite bible verses is Philippians 4:13 were it says;

"I can do all things through Christ who strengthens me."

Philippians 4:13 NKJV

Remember that it is your passion for life that will create your purpose in life.

In July 1991, I began to take food to the street corner of Colby and Hewitt in the city of Everett every Friday night from 5:00 to 8:00 PM to feed the homeless and hungry individuals and families that were living on the streets. I remember the month well; it was the beginning of July 1991. As I was watching the local news broadcast, over the past several days I couldn't help, but notice the homeless and hungry men, women and children who were living on the streets of Everett, Washington. They didn't know where their next meal was coming from. They didn't know when, and at times if there was another one coming at all. After watching several late-night news broadcasts of this same story, frustration started to arise inside of me. I tried to shake it out of my mind, but night after night it just kept coming back repeatedly. I didn't know it, but at that moment my purpose was being birthed and a passion ignited! I decided I wanted to live a life serving with my "palms down and not my palms up". It was time to make a move!

"For even the Son of Man did not come expecting to be served but to serve and give his life in exchange for the salvation of many.""

Matthew 20:28 TPT

A compassion and a call to action continued to burn in my heart for the men, women and children who are homeless. I began to wonder, what if this was me sleeping at bus stops, railroad track, in the woods of high growth areas, on the street corners, under freeways, in alleys, beside or behind dumpsters and garbage cans every single day? What would my prayer be? It would sound like this, "Lord, bless someone to give me a fresh meal today without judging me by looking at the current position I am in." I quickly realized that I could not change the whole world, but I could change my world! And once my world changes by giving out one meal, I could have a great impact on the lives of others in need! At that moment I realized that "the greater my collision was with people the greater the impact would be". The homeless and hungry were so scattered through-out the streets in the city of Everett that I knew in my heart what was needed, which was; someone to lead or Shephard them that they could trust not just for one meal, which is not a bad idea, but for a consistent meal every week. I wasn't interested in bringing religion to the streets, but I was very excited about building a relationship with the homeless and hungry that were living on the streets.

> "Then Jesus went about all the cities and villages, teaching in their synagogues, preaching the gospel of the kingdom, and healing every sickness and every disease among the people. But when He saw the multitudes, He was moved with compassion for them, because they were weary and scattered, like sheep having no shepherd. Then He said to His disciples, "The harvest truly is plentiful, but the laborers are few. "Therefore, pray the Lord of the harvest to send out laborers into His harvest."

Matthew 9:35-38 NKJV

The time had come for me to live my life as a distribution center. I was authorized and ready to make a difference in someone's life! I also knew at that moment that "I couldn't change the whole world, but I could change my world and everyone that I will encounter will experience a life changing experience. The time had also come to make disciples. What is a disciple? A student of a teacher or one that discipline.

"Students are not greater than their teacher. But the student who is fully trained will become like the teacher."

Luke 6:40 NLT

"He quoted a proverb: '"Can a blind man guide a blind man?' Wouldn't they both end up in the ditch? An apprentice doesn't lecture the master. The point is to be careful who you follow as your teacher."

Luke 6:39-40 MSG

The goal as a disciple (A student of a teacher) is to become like Jesus by studying His word and walking it out in your daily life. The goal also, is for discipleship to produce more disciples with the Gospel through developing disciples making leaders. We are called to fulfill the great commission and "Go" make disciples. Making disciples is not about having a biblical degree not that anything is wrong with obtaining higher education, as a matter a fact, I strongly encourage every person to enroll in a program that you're passionate about, so that your knowledge can be enhanced. Making disciples is more about a willingness to answer the call to follow Jesus, which is the only requirement to be a disciple of Jesus. Over the years, many individuals have asked me this particular question, "Can God use me to share the gospel?" My response is always the same, yes, He can use anyone that is faithful, available, and teachable. The reality is that curriculum, programs, and classes don't make disciples. Disciples make disciples, so what God really needs is YOU! Jesus did not live by methods; He lived the message before them daily. He was the message and the method. It is also very important that you live what you teach and preach, so others can see that you are living your message and methods as well, because the people you are disciplining can follow your life example. You will always reproduce what you are.

> *2 The only letter of recommendation we need is you yourselves. Your lives are a letter written in our hearts; everyone can read it and recognize our good work among you."*

2 Corinthians 3:2 NLT

> *11 I want you to pattern your lives after me, just as I pattern mine after Christ."*

1 Corinthians 11:1 TPT

Jesus was intimately involved in the lives of His disciples as they followed Him. He sacrificed His time, energy, and emotions in others, and since we are imitators of Jesus, we are called to follow His steps. One of the main reasons that disciples are not being made today is because most people realize that it takes a lot of commitment to walk people through the bible. Jesus' method of making disciples was focused more on relationship and action not just information and knowledge. Jesus gave all the disciples work to do. The disciples were developed in ministry by doing the work, through hands on experience. Whenever the disciples had a question regarding what happened on a ministry assignment they had just returned from, Jesus always had an answer for them. This allowed time for the disciples to reflect, review and to receive instructions from the teacher. Jesus did not micro-manage the disciples, He allowed them to make mistakes and instruct them on how they can correct it through empowering and equipping them to continue to 'GO" out and do it again.

To build His first leadership team, Jesus chose productive people and not professional religious leaders. He chose people that were already engaged in some type of productive activity. Many of them were entrepreneurs. When developing a leadership team, it may be wise to look for productive people and not just people who are professionals. Professional people are important for certain tasks however, productive people tend to get the job done because of their mindset. Productive people can be trained and developed into professional people, therefore, look to add productive people to your team. You can always train a productive person to be a professional. It is much more difficult to develop a professional person into a productive person if they were not that before they became professional. Productive is "achieving or producing a significant amount or result."

The Greek word used to describe a 'disciple' is *mathetes*, which describes a student or an individual who is learning from another in a mentor-like relationship. The person who is a *mathetes* is learning from the individual whom they are following. When Jesus Christ initially called His disciples to Him, He called them into a discipleship relationship. He was teaching them His ways and helping to instruct them in what God expected of them. As time went on, the Disciples began to understand and learn more of the word of God, until it became time to send them out as messengers to take the gospel to the world. In Luke 9:1, Christ calls His disciples together and gives them authority over the spirit world, and the authority to heal diseases, and then sends them out to preach the good news which is the Gospel and to heal the sick.

> *"9 Then He called His twelve disciples together and gave them power and authority over all demons, and to cure diseases."*

Luke 9:1 NKJV

Luke 9:1 doesn't specifically reference the 12 disciples as apostles, but the parallel scripture in Matthew 10 does.

The Twelve Apostles

> *10 And when He had called His twelve disciples to Him, He gave them power over unclean spirits, to cast them out, and to heal all kinds of sickness and all kinds of disease. 2 Now the names of the twelve apostles are these: first, Simon, who is called Peter, and Andrew his brother; James the son of Zebedee, and John his brother; 3 Philip and Bartholomew; Thomas and Matthew the tax collector; James the son of Alphaeus, and Lebbaeus, whose surname was Thaddaeus; 4 Simon the Cananite, and Judas Iscariot, who also betrayed Him."*

The Greek word for "apostle" is *apostolos* which is used to convey someone being sent out for a specific purpose or goal. So, when the disciples were called to Christ in Matthew 10:1-4 and Luke 9:1 and given specific objectives to go out and preach the gospel to the world, they became *apostolos*, or apostles—in addition to being disciples.

The following scripture have been my disciple making scripture for over 30 years and counting,

> *28Go therefore and make disciples of all the nations, baptizing them in the name of the Father and of the Son and of the Holy Spirit,"*

Matthew 28:19 NKJV

Evangelism is not a suggestion from Jesus, it is a commandment as seen through out the four Gospels referring to the Great Commission.

THE WORD "GO"

> ***19 Go** therefore and make disciples of all the nations, baptizing them in the name of the Father and of the Son and of the Holy Spirit,"*

Matthew 28:19 NKJV

Now the first word that Jesus said to His disciples regarding "sharing the gospel" was the word "Go" which is an action word, it means just don't stand or sit still and turn into a monument, but to have continual movement which will

93

create momentum. Many born again believers that attend local churches today are just sitting on the premises instead of standing on the promises of Jesus when it comes to "Sharing the Gospel". Jesus said, "Go" which also means, as you are going you will make disciples. The same command that Jesus gave the disciples then, He has given us the same command to you and I today, which is to get up, go out and share the gospel. God's name is action, the first twoo letters are "G and O" which spells "GO" the last two letters backwards are "D and O" which spells "DO".

GOD = Go and DO = Action

GO – It's your responsibility as a believer in Jesus, to evangelize the world according to your ability and direction from God. You should never make an excuse, why you cannot share the gospel and evangelize your community, city, state, or world.

Did you know that there are many believers that have been hearing the word of God taught and preached, concerning sharing the Gospel, but refuse to activate the word they have heard, the following scripture tells us to not just be a hearer, but be a doer and if we don't do what has been commanded of us to do then it's a sin.

22 But be doers of the word, and not hearers only, deceiving yourselves. "

James 1:22 NKJV

17 Therefore, to him who knows to do good and does not do it, to him it is sin.

James 4:17 NKJV

The devil will try to consistently distract you with a spirit of busyness by not allowing you to get up and share the gospel. As I stated earlier, there are many born again believers that are just sitting on the church premises not sharing the gospel, which is a strategy from the Satan himself. The first three letters in Satan are "S.A.T." which spells "SAT". The enemy will not only try to turn your movement into a monument, but will also enlist you to be part of the chosen frozen group that refuses to share the gospel, but I declare and decree today that every born-again believer needs to get up out of their seat and on their feet and get in the streets and start sharing the Gospel. You might be thinking by now, Dr. Hampton I'm not a license minister and have not been given the ministerial gift as an evangelist, so how can I go share the Gospel? I'm so glad you asked the question, but I'm going to answer you back with a question, did you know that there are absolutely no excuses why you should not be sharing the Gospel. Let me explain it this way to you, and I really want you to attentively hear me. Remember the day, date and or time you accepted Jesus into your heart and made the decision that Jesus is now in control of your life? I'm glad you remember, well I want you to know that is the day you started to be spiritually educated, equipped, and empowered with everything that you need to share the Gospel. Let's look at Acts chapter four verse thirteen:

> *13 Now when they saw the boldness of Peter and John, and perceived that they were uneducated and untrained men, they marveled. And they realized that they had been with Jesus."*

Acts 4:13 NKJV

The preceding scriptural text confirms that it's not just your secular degree, but ultimately, it's your spiritual degree that qualifies you to go share the gospel and make disciples. The moment you receive Jesus into your heart is also the moment you also receive your **B.A.** because you were **"Born Again"**, your **master's** because you were touched by the **"Master Jesus"** and your **PHD** because you now have the **P**ower of the **H**oly Spirit and have been **D**elivered. So why are you waiting for a title from your local or any church. There have been many men and women that have received titles to teach and preach the Gospel, but refuse to activate the word that they are carrying. If Jesus' mother, Mary would have just carried the word, which was Jesus Himself, but never delivered the word she carried, there would be no Gospel to share, but since she delivered the word she was carrying, everyone of us was able to hear the Gospel to receive Jesus. Now, you are authorized to not just carry the word, but deliver the word you are carrying. Individuals with ties also need to realize and understand that before you become a deacon, minister, elder or pastor etc. You are first a soul winner then a deacon, a soul winner then a minister, a soul winner then a pastor. By now someone might be saying Dr. Hampton, "I'm a missionary?" My answer for you is, then go do missionary work. Jesus also shows us another outreach text in Acts chapter one verse two where it says.

"2 until the day in which He was taken up, after He through the Holy Spirit had given commandments to the apostles whom He had chosen,"

Acts 1:2 NKJV

The preceding scripture which is in connection with Matthew 28:19, is showing us that after Jesus gave the command to the apostles to "Go and make disciples". He then left the scene to go be with His father

THE WORD "THEREFORE"

*"19 Go **therefore** and make disciples of all the nations, baptizing them in the name of the Father and of the Son and of the Holy Spirit,"*

Matthew 28:19 NKJV

The meaning of the word "therefore" means that you have been authorized to go preach and teach the gospel. What does the word power of attorney mean? It is the legal and written authority to transact business for another. A person can be a general agent to represent another in all his/her business, or a special agent who is authorized to do some specific work or transact some special business. The agent can act with all authority within the bounds of the legal authorization as much as the one who gave them the authority.

When looking at the great commission, there are four words that standout; **Go**, **teach**, **baptize all disciples** and **teach**.

The word "Go" applies to all believers not only preachers. The invitation to salvation is for everyone, so why should it not be the responsibility of the believer to offer the invitation of salvation everyone. We have the same rights and privileges, promises and provision for equipping for service, so everyone should help in every possible way to evangelize the world according to their ability and direction from God. There is no excuse for millions of church members leaving this type of work to only a few who seek to be obedient to the great commission. To teach is the Greek word," matheteuo" which means to make disciples, enroll as a student. This is not the same meaning as the word "teaching" in this text. The word teaching in the text means to give instruction rather than enrolling a student to be taught, ..."in the name of" means the authority of which is by the authority of all three persons and not by the authority of Jesus only. He is the one authorizing us to recognize the others as well as himself. It is by the authority of Jesus Christ that we are baptized at all, and it is by His authority that we baptize in the name of the authority of all three persons. The Scripture says the father and of the son and of the Holy Spirit. Some people will argue that these are not names, but the dictionary said that the word name is "any word" or "title" by which any person or thing is known. This is not just any father, any son or any Holy Spirit, but it is the father of Jesus Christ and the son of the father and the Holy Spirit the third person of the divine Trinity.

> *"And He said to them, "As you go into all the world, preach openly the wonderful news of the gospel to the entire human race!"*
>
> **Mark 16:15 TPT**

"You can do evangelism with excellence and in return excellence will always promote itself" —Dr. Ray Hampton

Evangelism is not about being perfect, it's about excellence. Being perfect will not allow you to make mistakes, but having excellence will push you past your mistakes. Mistakes are only mistakes if you keep making the same mistakes, but when you learn from your mistakes, it's a learning experience. Evangelism is the backbone or spine of the local church and when your physical back hurts it will affect how your whole body feels, so it is the same with the church. If there is no evangelism in the local church, the church is affected. If the local church does not have a children's ministry or outreach ministry the church is either starting to decline or in stagnation. Why? Because there are no children growing up and no one coming in, which means that everyone is getting older in age and preparing for heavenly promotion. If the local church fails to support the ministry of evangelism, it will be the cause of a lack of growth in the local church, which ultimately will have a negative impact on the expansion of the kingdom of God. As a verb, the word *evangelism* is an expression meaning," to announce good news'. When an individual has been evangelized, it means that they have been made aware. The Greek word for gospel is "evangelion" which means "Good News", the Greek word for "preach" is "evanggelizo" which means "to bring good news". The Greek word for "evangelist" is "evagglistes" which means, "one who declares good news". The purpose for evangelism is not for you to try to convince or convert someone to salvation, but to share the gospel of Jesus Christ with them. Jesus wants you to be an effective witness for Him not a Judge. Your assignment as a believer is to love God, love people and share your faith experience. Evangelism is not just church work, it is ultimately kingdom work, why? Because it is not based on how many people that the local church has retained, but how many that the local church is sending out. Retaining people in church will cause stagnation in the growth of the ministry, which will cause the local church to turn into a monument that will always stop movement. Evangelism is about movement. The community, city and the world will financially support the local church because of evangelism. Most churches don't have a financial problem, what they are experiencing is a people (Fish) problem.

Matthew 17:27 NKJV

When Jesus saw Peter and his brother Andrew, He made the following statement in scripture.

Matthew 4:18-20 NKJV

The phrases "follow me" and "left their nets" are known as idioms. An idiom is a group of words in a fixed order that have a particular meaning that is different from the meanings of each word on its own. Idioms add color to the language and makes it more effective and interesting to the listeners.

Example:

Idiom: "You have bitten off more than you can chew"

Meaning: "You have tried to do something which is too difficult for you"

Idiom: "Don't let the grass grow under your feet"

Meaning: "Don't delay in getting something done"

The words "follow me" in verse nineteen is an idiom of "Discipleship" and "left their nets" or "leaving all" in verse twenty is an idiom of "Putting God first"

- ⊙ Evangelism is strategic and intentionally
- ⊙ Evangelism is about making a positive contact with others not contaminate them with negativity
- ⊙ Evangelism is not only about a method, but ultimately the message
- ⊙ Evangelism is not just about explaining, but it is also an experience
- ⊙ Evangelism is not about impressing people with material possessions, but to lead them in genuine confession
- ⊙ Evangelism is serving with your palms down and not your palms up
- ⊙ Evangelism is not just about giving a handout, but hand up
- ⊙ Evangelism is not only coming to church by yourself, but to bring someone with you
- ⊙ Evangelism is seeing the church as a soul winning station
- ⊙ Evangelism is seeing the local church as a spiritual hospital for sinners and not a night club for Christians
- ⊙ Evangelism is not about buildings, but about people

- Evangelism is about people that go and make disciples that grow
- Evangelism is not goal driven, but people driven
- Evangelism is loving God and loving people
- Evangelism is teaching and practicing which is relaying a message to another individual, but doing outreach is coaching, how are you going to coach what you have not taught?
- Evangelism is about being committed not comfortable. A lot of Christians want to be comfortable, but very few want to be committed.
- Evangelism is the process to see the results
- Evangelism is not just about elevation, but ultimately, it's all about acceleration. Many people are elevated by titles, but never go out and do the work.
- Evangelism is not about building a religion, but a relationship with people
- Evangelism is not about a church building campaign, but about creating a culture of evangelism within the church
- Evangelism is telling others your story and discipleship is you listening to their story
- Evangelism always starts with your life and not your words

*"But you shall receive power when the Holy Spirit has come upon you;
and you shall be witnesses to Me in Jerusalem, and in all Judea and
Samaria, and to the end of the earth.""*

Acts 1:8 NKJV

It amazes me how many people don't want to be a
witness, but will do witnessing. The above text doesn't say
anything about doing witnessing, but says a lot about being a
witness. Doing without being doesn't make disciples. Being a
witness means that you have been authorized by Jesus Christ
to "Go Make Disciples".

For over 30 years, I've been asked this particular question
by thousands of people, "How can I change the lives of
individuals?" My answer has always been "by reaching one
person at a time". "If you try to reach the thousands you might
miss the one, but if you touch the one you will reach the
thousands!" You can expand beyond your borders to reach
tens of thousands of people not by just giving a handout, but
a hand up to the men, women and children who are homeless
and hungry.

There are many times in life that I'm sure you needed to
do something that you felt passionate about, but because of a
lack of finances and hanging around negative thinking
individuals, doubt started to set in, but my advice to you is to
do what the word says,

"Trust in and rely confidently on the Lord with all your heart and do not rely on your own insight or understanding. In all your ways know and acknowledge and recognize Him, And He will make your paths straight and smooth [removing obstacles that block your way]."

Proverbs 3:5-6 AMP

There must be a trust in what I am passionate about for everything to work out for my purpose. I need to trust God from the bottom of my heart and stop trying to figure out everything on my own.

During the time I was feeding on the streets my family, I was a member of the Powerhouse Church of God in Christ where Henry Jenkins was the pastor. Every weekend while I was a member of the church, I would see one of the preachers Elder Craig Jackson who also was a successful business owner of Ribbons Barbeque in Ballard, preach on the corner of multiple streets. In Mark 16:15, street preaching is seen as a commandment from Jesus as a way to warn people about sins and their consequences. This is supported by Isaiah 58:1 and Jeremiah 2:2.

"And He said to them, "Go into all the world and preach the gospel to every creature."

Mark 16:15 NKJV

""Cry aloud, spare not; Lift up your voice like a trumpet; Tell My people their transgression, And the house of Jacob their sins."

Isaiah 58:1 NKJV

105

"God's Message came to me. It went like this: "Get out in the streets and call to Jerusalem, 'God's Message! I remember your youthful loyalty, our love as newlyweds. You stayed with me through the wilderness years, stuck with me through all the hard places."

Jeremiah 2:1-2 MSG

A father and son were driving down the streets and as they were riding in the car, they encountered a man preaching on the streets. The son said to his father, why is he speaking loud to the people, but no one is listening?" The father replied to his son, "did you hear him? The son replied yes.

Even though Craig Jackson was responsible for a thriving business with lots of employees, every weekend he would still always grab his Lone Ranger speaker system and go to the street corner to preach throughout the city.

One Sunday after church, I shared with Craig Jackson how I wanted to go with him to go help on the streets of Seattle in any way that I could. After going multiple times, the confirmation was in my heart to start an outreach ministry and in July 1991 the street ministry was birth in the city of Everett.

I began to feed on the street corner of Colby and Hewitt in Everett, Washington every Friday night from 5:00-8: 00pm.When I started feeding, I didn't have any equipment at all, but some amazing things began to happen for the ministry. Before I knew it someone had donated a card table to put the food on and even though it had one weak leg, it still was workable. Don't laugh about the weak leg, at least it was a workable leg. The owner of McDonald's in south Everett on 128th street had donated a ten-gallon red and yellow McDonald Jug, and over thirty years later, can you believe I still have the same ten-gallon McDonald Jug container and it has served millions of drinks to many hungry and homeless individuals. Even though the table had a weak leg it was still able to hold the sandwiches and the ten-gallon water container. There was a bakery in Everett call Gai's bakery that donated loaves of bread and Safeway on Broadway donated the bologna to feed the homeless and hungry. I've learned the best way to receive what you need for your ministry is to ask for it. If you get a "no", eventually you will get a yes if you keep on knocking. Effective prayer and persistence are going to be two major keys that will open doors for you to succeed in whatever you have been called to do.

"Ask, and the gift is yours. Seek, and you'll discover. Knock, and the door will be opened for you. For every persistent one will get what he asks for. Every persistent seeker will discover what he longs for. And everyone who knocks persistently will one day find an open door."

Matthew 7:7-8 TPT

There are many forms of prayer. The first major type of prayer is Talking to God which is a form of "Conversational" prayer or "Dialogical" prayer; which is the most common type of prayer. The second, major type of prayer is called "Contemplative" prayer or "Silent" Prayer.

When you are praying, you are not only communicating with God which is upward prayer, but also you are exploring your relationship with God through your inward prayer and for other people it's an outward prayer. Internal dialogical prayer includes areas which correspond to upward (God), inward (Self), and outward (others) prayer.

> *"I tell you, even though he will not get up and give him anything just because he is his friend, yet because of his persistence and boldness he will get up and give him whatever he needs."*

Luke 11:8 AMP

In the Scriptures right before Luke 11:8, Jesus talks about the importance of being persistent, Jesus is telling His disciples that if they pray long enough and are persistent enough, God will give them what they're asking for. Let's take a look at the following text.

> *"Then He said to them, "Suppose one of you has a friend, and goes to him at midnight and says, 'Friend, lend me three loaves [of bread]; for a friend of mine who is on a journey has just come to visit me, and I have nothing to serve him'; and from inside he answers, 'Do not bother me; the door has already been shut and my children and I are in bed; I cannot get up and give you anything.'"*

Luke 11:5-7 AMP

Let's now look at the conclusion of what happens when you pray and is persistent.

""So, I say to you, ask and keep on asking, and it will be given to you; seek and keep on seeking, and you will find; knock and keep on knocking, and the door will be opened to you. For everyone who keeps on asking [persistently], receives; and he who keeps on seeking [persistently], finds; and to him who keeps on knocking [persistently], the door will be opened."

Luke 11:9-10 AMP

As you're reading about the items and might be wondering what else I had, such as money or someone that financed the start of the ministry. Well, here's your answer. I didn't have any personal startup money and did not ask for anyone to give me any money. No one in the city even knew my name and I didn't have a track record for doing any type of non-profit or profit types of business, but you know what I did have? A great G. P.A. which was a Goal, Passion, Action and of course, a dream.

Goal the object of a person's ambition or effort, or it can be an aim or desire result.

PASSION - When you are passionate for someone or something you will have an intense emotional excitement. You will always have a continued zeal, strong desire, feeling toward something or someone which causes a craving and stirring up within yourself.

PERSISTENCE – Your persistency will show you're patient toward a certain goal even when you are faced with opposition and going through adversity;

109

you refuse to give up, cave in or quit because of the endurance within you to bear the pain without flinching.

PRODUCTIVITY – Fertilization will always bring fruit, because of your productivity. It is the act of producing or the giving and putting out your effort to see an increasing product to realization.

PRODUCE – To produce means that you have given life to something or someone and now you have a cause and effect of a product. The product is the result of your productivity and will cause birth to a production of something else.

Action is the fact or process of doing something typically to achieve an aim

As you're reading my story, my question is what's your story? Why are you still waiting for someone to give you a handout when Jesus has already given you a hand up? There is no greater hand you can hold on to that will guide you on your journey, of the ministry assignment that has been given to you like Jesus can. God has not forgotten about you!

> *[29] For the gifts and the calling of God are irrevocable [for He does not withdraw what He has given, nor does He change His mind about those to whom He gives His grace or to whom He sends His call.* **Romans 11:29 AMP**

Always remember this, "When you do what He tells you to do your harvest will always come.

2 1-3 Three days later there was a wedding in the village of Cana in Galilee. Jesus' mother was there. Jesus and his disciples were guests also. When they started running low on wine at the wedding banquet, Jesus' mother told him, "They're just about out of wine."

4 Jesus said, "Is that any of our business, Mother—yours or mine? This isn't my time. Don't push me."

*5 She went ahead anyway, telling the servants, **"Whatever he tells you, do it."***

6-7 Six stoneware water pots were there, used by the Jews for ritual washings. Each held twenty to thirty gallons. Jesus ordered the servants, "Fill the pots with water." And they filled them to the brim.

*8 "Now fill your pitchers and take them to the host," Jesus said, **and they did.***

*9-10 When the host tasted the water that had become wine (**he didn't know what had just happened but the servants, of course, knew**), he called out to the bridegroom, "Everybody I know begins with their finest wines and after the guests have had their fill brings in the cheap stuff. But you've saved the best till now!"*

John 2:1-10 MSG

It doesn't matter if its spiritual, physical, or financial, believe me when I say that I have experienced all three harvests, every harvest has come my way, because of the consistency that I have done throughout the years. I didn't start with a lot, but I'm receiving His blessings every day.

"And though you started with little, you will end with much."

Job 8:7 NLT

In a short amount of time, the Ray Hampton Outreach Ministries Street evangelism made such an impact throughout the city that The Seattle Times wrote a newspaper article about what was happening.

EVERETT CORNER OUTDOOR PULPIT FOR PREACHER
Man takes to downtown streets to try to reach troubled teenagers

Everett - Saturday night, corner of Hewitt and Colby. Five disaffected kids holding up a deli wall, two haggard men lost to their own ramblings, and now, one preacher with the PA system. "You don't have to be walking up and down the streets," intones Raymond Hampton lll, doing just that in Gray suit, a tie and a James Brown rasp. "You can FIND somewhere to go in Jesus! He'll be your friend!" A bearded man in a baseball cap leans into a phone booth, steps away, making call after call. A girl in a red fishnet top walks by dragging on a cigarette, makeup smudge on her hard face. She spies the bearded man and the toughness crumbles; they exclaim and hug each other, rocking wordlessly back and forth. "JESUS!" Hampton sings. "Can-ya-say JESUS!!"

Hampton, 26, is not discouraged. It's only been three weeks since he moved his street preaching from the gang held corners of Seattle to downtown Everett, his home city. The audience here is much milder. But a racial harassment incident last month convinced Hampton that Everett needs healing, too. Snohomish County prosecutors last week declined to file charges in the incident, in which Hampton and his 4-year- old son were verbally threatened and insulted for 20 minutes outside an Everett supermarket by a man who said he was a white supremacist. Frustrated, Hampton decided to channel his anger into something positive. His preaching warns the street crowd against drugs, alcohol and gains, sometimes drawing derisive comments from the audience. "Hey, I like it when they say 'shut up', I like it when they flip me off," Hampton said, "because at least I know they heard me, they heard me."

Next week Hampton plans to set up a long picnic table with cookies and pop on the corner, "because these kids are hungry," he said. He also plans to preach outside Club Vogue, a nearby teen club. A group of teenagers, the same every weekend, arrive at the corner by bus, car, skateboard. They do little other than stare at the passers-by, grind cigarettes into the pavement and keep one ear to the pay phone, which Hampton says is used to sell drugs. "They don't give us nothing to do, so we gotta come down here and get into trouble," says Anthony,

17. He said Club Vogue wasn't his cup of tea. Some recent Hampton's intrusion. "I think he better get the hell off my avenue," snorts Claudette, 18, with spiky red hair and fresh cuts on her wrist. She waits by the phone, shaking in her leather jacket. An older man who says he's been off drugs for three months, quietly approaches Hampton and tells him to keep preaching. So, does a man in a floppy hat who's portable stereo blares Latin music. Police keep a watchful eye on the corner, but leave Hampton to his own devices. About 9:00 PM, patrolman Robert Whidbey, with a warm smile and firm handshake, wades into the crowd to warn them about the city's loitering law. "I'm not asking you to leave now, but I'm letting you know I can do that," he says; the group is not impressed. Whidbey shakes his head at Hampton, still gesticulating, "While this is a problem area, don't think I will confront the problem on my own like this," he says before heading back to his patrol car. Everett police report little organized gang activity, but are aware it's moving north from Seattle and Tacoma. Indeed, some people identify several bands of youth occupying downtown street corners after hours as "folks," nickname for the local Black Gangster Disciples.

Street ministry, too, is developing. Operation night watch, a group of ministers who interact with "night people" Taverns and on the street in Seattle, Tacoma and Spokane, abandoned its Everett campaign two years ago, said director

Norm Riggins. The ministry couldn't find enough volunteers in local churches. "I just know the need is there to stay in touch with that community," Riggins said. "these guys and gals on the street can't just go into church and sit next to someone in a fur coat. You have got to go to them." A youth group of self-professed former drug dealers from a local fundamentalist church recently preached to Street kids on Hewitt and Colby corner. They showed up Saturday night to compare notes with Hampton. As the preaching wound down, a man in a floppy hat approach Hampton one more time. "I hope you save some people, cuz I'm going to hell myself," he said. He waited for that to sink in, then let the salsa beat carry him across the street.

The Seattle Times Newspaper

So much was going on that summer, my wife and I was expecting our fifth child, he was delivered on August 7, 1991, and was named "Isaiah Cornelius Hampton". He was born with down syndrome, something that my wife and I never experienced with our other children. So, immediately we knew that this was going to be a life changing experience. After weekly and monthly hospital visits to the hospital regarding Isaiah, he was eventually hospitalized in December of that year where my wife and I had to learn to feed him twenty-four calorie milk due to his lack of growth. In January 1992, on a Friday night, I was sitting at a night service holding Isaiah during praise and worship service and tears began to run down my face as I was feeling something strong in my spirit. Even though I didn't know why I was feeling the way I was, my spirit felt very heavy, as I was sitting on the back row, I signaled for Pastor Henry Jenkins to come and pray for Isaiah. Two days later early one morning around 2:00am, I got out of bed to check on Isaiah in his crib and noticed that he was not responding, I immediately shouted for my wife to get up and I will never forget the words that she said with a loud voice "OH MY BABY". The aid car was immediately called, and I remember them running upstairs and once they were in the room, they immediately started to try to revive him and then began wrapping Isaiah up to take him to the ambulance to try to revive him even more. My wife and I rushed downstairs to get into our car to go to the hospital, once we arrived there we were immediately escorted to the room where Isaiah was. I will never forget the feeling I had as my eyes filled up with tears when I saw my young son Isaiah laying on the bed not moving at all, the doctor approached me and said, 'Mr. Hampton I'm so sorry." I was so angry at that because I felt my world had been turned upside down, my son was no longer here with us. We eventually began planning Isaiah's service. One of the greatest things that happened during Isaiah's homegoing celebration (Funeral) was that my wife's' oldest brother, Eddie Cornelius Boyd gave his heart to the Lord and three weeks later, he transitioned to go live with Jesus. Again, my wife was hit with another lost and then three months later her mom, Lucille Boyd or as she was known to many in the Church Mother Boyd, transitioned to live with Jesus as well. As you can see, we went through a lot as a family and even though many tears flowed day, nights, weeks, months and even now as I'm writing this book, my eyes are starting to become unfocused because of the tears that are getting ready to flow. There's not a day that goes by that I don't think about the months of January to May the year of 1992. Even though I miss my son dearly, have cried many tears probably enough to fill an ocean and have visited Isaiah's grave site, I'm reminded of few scriptures.

> *14 But Jesus said, "Let the little children come to Me, and do not forbid them; for of such is the kingdom of heaven."*
>
> **Matthew 19:14 NKJV**

> *8 We are confident, yes, well pleased rather to be absent from the body and to be present with the Lord.*
>
> **2 Corinthians 5:8 NKJV**

> *15 Precious in the sight of the LORD Is the death of His saints.*
>
> **Psalms 116:15 NKJV**

Even though my wife and I went through a lot, we continued to keep our faith in God. We continued to go to church at the Powerhouse Church of God in Christ.

Over a period of months, I was watching a commercial on TV from Jack Roberts Appliance who was known for his saying "I won't be undersold". After hearing this repeatedly day after day, I decided to go stop by the appliance store located in Lynnwood, WA. and ask to speak to the owner, Jack Roberts. The front desk receptionist paged him to come to the front lobby because a guest was waiting for him. When Jack arrived in the lobby, I will never forget the look on his face when he greeted me and said, "Aren't you the one that is feeding on the streets in downtown Everett?" My response was, "yes, I am." He said, "how can I help you?" I began to explain to him how I needed a vehicle to transport food from the stores to take to the streets. Without hesitation, his response was "let's do it." After weeks of looking for a vehicle, we ended up finding a ford passenger bus in Oak Harbor, Washington with a two-speed rear in. After the bus was purchased, I went back to say thank you to Jack Roberts and received the news of my life. He said to me and I quote, "As long as you keep serving the hungry and homeless on the streets, you can stop by here every other Friday for the next two years and pick up a check for $500.00 for your mission." I was so excited to know that again where God guides, he provides. Now, I had a forty-passenger bus and guaranteed funding for the ministry for the next two years and felt like I could conquer the world by feeding everywhere. One day I was driving the bus, and someone asked me, "When did you get your CDL?" My answer was, "what is a CDL?" They responded by saying it's a Commercial Driver's License. Not realizing I had been driving illegally I immediately called the local Department of License about getting my Commercial Driver License, but before I could go take the test, God showed up again. My cousin Ossha, who was living in our home at the time and attending Mariner High School in Everett, Washington had a friend named Tessa who came home with Ossha just to hang out. One day, Tessa's dad came to pick up his daughter, but while we were talking, he remember me from years ago playing open gym basketball at Lynnwood Junior High school. He said, "Is that your bus that's always driving around?" I said yes, it is. He said, "Where did you get your CDL?" At this time, I was thinking in my mind, here we go again... but I said, "I don't have one." Not knowing what his response would be, not that it mattered to me because I was scheduled to go get one. As he continued to talk, the next group of words that came out of his mouth, was life changing. He said, "I work for Snohomish County City Transit and in charge of the testing for our drivers, I can give you a test, are you ready now?" What do you think I said? YES! After going for a lengthy drive, he signed the test paper, then I took it to the Department of License and guess what endorsement they put on your Driver's License? You guessed right... A COMMERCIAL DRIVERS LICENSE! God did it again and at the time of this writing of A PASSION FOR A PURPOSE, I have now had my Commercial Driver's License for over thirty-years. Again, wherever God guides, He provides! Or can I say this way, where there is God's will, there's a way! I think you get the point. "Where there is God's WILL there's a RAY".

> 28 *And we know [with great confidence] that God [who is deeply concerned about us] causes all things to work together [as a plan] for good for those who love God, to those who are called according to His plan and purpose.*

Romans 8:28 AMP

As I've already stated, the subtitle for this book "Taking it to the Streets" which is "A passion for purpose" and the above scripture will remind you daily that God has a plan and purpose for your life as long as you will stay in love with Him. Three months after my son Isaiah transitioned to go live with Jesus, God continued to bless Ray Hampton Outreach Ministries. I realized all I had to do is continue to do as the scripture says.

> 7 *for we walk by faith, not by sight [living our lives in a manner consistent with our confident belief in God's promises]*

2 Corinthians 5:7 AMP

In May 1992, Elder Craig Jackson started a church "king of Glory Worldwide Ministries Church of God in Christ" in Skyway next door to 7'11 which means that he was no longer going to be a member of the "Powerhouse Church of God in Christ". After much prayer, my family and I started to attend the king of Glory Church of God in Christ as one of the founding members. Since 1989, my wife and I had been driving from Everett to Seattle for multiple years and now we were getting ready to help plant a new church in the skyway area of Seattle. WOW! I remember how the first service was full, even though the building only held between 50 to 75 people at max capacity. I know you might be thinking to yourself, "that was a small building,". If you're thinking that, then my three questions to you are, how big was Jesus' building, what was His address and did Jesus have a mega-church or mega-mission? I been saying for over 30 years that Jesus was people focused not building focus. I'm not saying you shouldn't have a building for your church or ministry; all I'm saying is, make sure that you keep your focus on the main thing which is people! I knew from the moment that I met Elder Craig Jackson in 1989 at Powerhouse Church of God in Christ, from watching him preach with the anointing, yelling and screaming JESUS, jumping up and down doing praise and worship time. I have to stop right here and say this, Elder Craig Jackson could leap very high in the air and would land on both feet, get his balance and repeatedly do it over and over and over again. As you're reading this book and if you've ever visited or was a member at Powerhouse, you were there to witness what I'm

121

saying. If the ceiling was any lower, he would've jump right out of the building. Thank God for a 25-foot ceiling that had skylights. I knew in my heart as he continued to preach on the streets that he was going to do some amazing things one day to make a great impact in the Kingdom that God had given him, to maximize his calling that God had given him to do.

As the months continued to go by, my membership at King of Glory was short. Can you believe that I got an offer to be the Evangelism Pastor for a church that was closer to our home located in Lynnwood Washington that was called "Living Water Church" where Dave White was the senior pastor. The church congregation was about sixty to seventy people and the music was different than what I was used to, and I mean extremely different. I went from clapping on the second and fourth beat to clapping on the first and second beat. You see, in 1975 my parents moved the family from Holly Park in Seattle. I must be honest right here and say, that there was no diversity in the city, and I didn't see anyone who looked like me. There was no sugar hill gang music playing or The Jackson 5; not even a sneak sound of any Motown music playing, but there was a lot of Van Halen, AC/DC, Kiss, and the Eagles, I think by now you have gotten the point of what I'm saying. Well anyway, that was my environment from 6th grade at Evergreen Elementary School until I graduated from Lynnwood High School. As you have just read, I grew up as a child in the Edmonds school District, in the Montlake Terrace and the City of Lynnwood, so the beat wasn't new; it was just new for me to hear it in church. Well, let's get back to talking about what happened next in my life. I was so excited about the promotion that was getting ready to take place in my life. Something was getting ready to happen in my life that was going to be the start of an amazing Journey especially when it comes to being a paid staff at a church. I never would've imagined this ever happening mostly because I never have heard of anyone especially a minister, elder, missionary, musician or pastor getting paid to be on a staff at a Church. In my surroundings in Seattle, I've only had seen pastors receive finances from anniversary services and special offerings, but never on a repeated monthly staff position. Pastor Dave and I had many meetings about what he wanted to do in the Lynnwood area regarding reaching people for Christ, through evangelism and outreach. Through much prayer and fasting, himself and the board of Living Water Church felt that I was the man for the job. Well, I couldn't believe what was getting ready to happen for me and my family.

This was going to be my first paid staff position at $800 a month. The church wasn't diverse, but the people were awesome and had a heart for God and that's what really mattered to me. I spoke at the church multiple Sunday nights on evangelism to empower and equip the people and the church. In a few short months, the attendance began to grow. Pastor Dave was finally able to go on a vacation and left me in charge. That year in 1992, the local news stations reported that there was an arsonist that was going around different cities in Snohomish County setting churches on fire, and it wasn't Holy Spirit fire either, unfortunately the living water church was one of the targets of his fire spree. As Pastor Dave was on vacation, we had just finished a Sunday night service and the next day we had received the news that the Living Water Church had been burned down, which now caused the church to be in transition. Even though my time there was short spent I still had to maintain the calling that God had put on my life.

After a year and a half of serving the homeless, hopeless, and helpless on the streets I felt a strong tugging in my heart to start a church called Safe in his Arms Christian Center. Which was birthed on the first Sunday of November 1992 in the city of Everett at the Howard Johnson hotel. Believing by faith that the people I was serving on the streets will now have a place to call home in terms of when it comes to Church. Even though I was a licensed minister of the Church of God in Christ and not an ordained elder I wanted the church to be under the organization of the "Church of God in Christ". I remember there was a superintendent of the Church of God in Christ named Lee Young who also pastored a church in Everett and once he found out that I was starting a church, he asked me a question, "Is your church part of the Church of God in Christ?" The response to him was, no it's not. He continues to ask the next question, "why not?" And my response to that question was, "Because I'm not an ordained elder in the Church of God in Christ". Superintendent Lee Young then responded back to me with one last question, "Do you mind if I call Bishop to see what we can do to get you to be under Church of God in Christ". I told him that would be fine with me. He immediately called Bishop T.L. Westbrook who was the state prelate at that time and began to explain the conversation that we were currently having. For the next ten to twenty minutes, I listened in to the conversation that was taking place on the phone between Bishop Westbrook and Superintendent Young, about the evangelism and outreach that had been taking place in the Downtown area of Everett. Superintendent Young shared with him about all the people lives that had been change and souls that have been saved because of the Gospel in action, such as Feeding the Homeless, Hopeless and Helpless. He shared with the Bishop about the huge crowds of people that he had witnessed on the downtown street corner every Friday night. I remember thinking to myself, "here we go again!" The words of a song started ringing in my spirit which was, "You may not know how, you may not know when, but He will do it again". I knew that this was a special moment and God was using Superintendent Young to usher it in. While they were talking on the phone I was having church in the spirit. The Hammond B-3 was playing in E flat, the drums were on two and four, the bass and electric guitar was on point. If you have ever been to a Church of God in Christ service, you should already know that an anointed guitarist can add a lot to a church service. Can I get an AMEN! Well anyway, the song that was taking place was, "I got a feeling everything is going to be alright".

Days later, I received a phone call from Bishop T.L. Westbrook stating the fact that he had a Conversation with Superintendent Lee Young regarding me being a pastor in the Church of God in Christ and that Superintendent Young had talked about all the great works that had taken place in the ministry. To my amazement, Bishop Westbrook began to share with me that he had been watching me through-out the media, on the news for years regarding the work that was being done in serving the unfortunate throughout the city of Everett and if I was going to start a church that it would be an honor to have me to be part of the Church of God in Christ. Our conversation went as follows; Bishop Westbrook: "What church were you a member of in Church of God in Christ?" Me: "I was a member and licensed minister at the Powerhouse Church of God in Christ under Pastor Henry Jenkins." Bishop Westbrook: "What year did you get your Minister License?" Me: "December 1990." Bishop Westbrook: "Were you in good standing with the Pastor?" Me: "Yes Sir!" Bishop Westbrook: "OKay then. Well, I'm gonna contact Pastor Henry Jenkins and I'm going to get back to you, would it be okay if I call you at this number?" Me: "Yes sir!"

In less than one-week myphone rang and guess what? You're right, it was Bishop T.L. Westbrook, the Washington State Prelate of the Church of God in Christ. Now, in my spirit I began to sing again. If you have or are currently a member of the Church of God in Christ, c'mon and sing this next phrase with me... LET THE CHURCH SAY YES, YES, YES, YES LORD, YES LORD, YES LORD! Our phone conversation was life changing. Bishop Westbrook: "Hello preacher, well, I spoke to Jenkins, and He's given his approval and said that you were and honor to pastor, faithful in your tithes and offerings, never given him any problems, have a great outreach ministry and shared with me how you would bring a lot of people from your area to church every Sunday driving a big 40 passenger bus. I just think that is tremendous!" Me: "Thank you Bishop." Bishop: "Well, I would like to get you ordained as an Elder as soon as possible, are you okay with that?" Me: "Yes Sir!" Immediately a song started up in my spirit and before you put me on your judgement seat, I wasn't being rude while he was talking, I was very excited! C'mon, let's sing it together …. THIS IS THE CHURCH OF GOD IN CHRIST, THIS IS THE CHURCH OF GOD IN CHRIST, YOU CAN'T JOIN

IN YOU GOT TO BE BORN IN, THIS IS THE CHURCH OF GOD IN CHRIST! Bishop Westbrook stated to me that he wanted to ordain me, which was not through sitting in front of a board of superintendents and elders at the yearly convocation, but he wanted to set a date for my ordination service. On November 29,1992 at the Bible Way Church of God in Christ, I was ordained at the age of twenty-eight which made me the youngest elder that year in the state of Washington of the Church of God in Christ. I felt so honored to be ordained by men that have been well known for years such as Bishop T.L. Westbrook, First Administrator Assistant James Hicks, Secretary Edgar Gray and Pastor Henry Jenkins.

Over the next fourteen months, the Safe in His Arms Church of God in Christ rented multiple spaces moving from Howard Johnson Hotel, South Everett Christian Center and to the city of Snohomish on 3rd & Avenue B where I was told by the city that I was the first African-American pastor in the city and even though there were three moves in fourteen months "sometimes I felt like a failure and other times I felt like a champion excelling in life". The uniqueness about the church in the city of Snohomish was that it was going to be our own building. We didn't have a lot of money, but we had a lot hope, dreams, visions, and faith in God that He will allow it to be our building. I remember taking my father to look at this old vintage church building and to sit in on the meeting regarding the building. I met with the owner of the building, and he was so impressed on how the ministry was serving the homeless and hungry that were living on the streets that he immediately said that he wanted us in the building. So, within minutes we ended up our meeting, signing the contract to lease the building on a brown paper bag. Are you ready for the least amount? Well, God did it again. We were able to lease the building for $800 a month.

The blessings of God continued to come so fast that it reminded me of the following scripture;

> 13-15 *"Yes indeed, it won't be long now." GOD's Decree._"Things are going to happen so fast your head will swim, one thing fast on the heels of the other. You won't be able to keep up. Everything will be happening at once—and everywhere you look, blessings! Blessings like wine pouring off the mountains and hills. I'll make everything right again for my people Israel:*
>
> *"They'll rebuild their ruined cities. They'll plant vineyards and drink good wine. They'll work their gardens and eat fresh vegetables. And I'll plant them, plant them on their own land._They'll never again be uprooted from the land I've given them."*
> *GOD, your God, says so.*

Amos 9:13-15 MSG.

God blessed the ministry with our very own bus to transport the homeless and hungry as well as pick up food and other items that we might need. I would like to take a pause right here and share something with you. If you keep on being consistent in the ministry assignment that God has given you and don't get distracted by chasing material possessions, but continue to chase after God, He knows what you need before you ask. All He's looking for is your obedience to the assignment He has given you. This next newspaper article is going to share with you what God did for us even after everything we had been through, God set His stamp of approval and blesses Ray Hampton Outreach Ministry again!

ON THE MOVE
Pastor stands up to adversity; takes message to the street

"We're going to the helpless, the hopeless and the homeless"

Raymond Hampton III; he's always looking ahead, thinking big. Take an old school bus for example. To others, it may be an old well past its prime. For Hampton, it's a gift from God. "I'll fix it up a bit, slap a billboard on the side and set up an electric power and drum machine inside. it'll be a mobile church," says Hampton, who plans to cruise the streets of downtown Everett in his bus and preach the gospel to anyone willing to listen, bringing a new meaning to the term Street preacher. "We're going to the helpless, the hopeless and the homeless." says the 27-year-old, speaking with the tone of a Pentecostal and the craftiness of a salesman. The fact is, he's both. On one hand, Hampton is pastor of Safe in his Arms Church of God in Christ, a Pentecostal congregation he organized several months ago that attracts about 20 people a week, services are held at the West Coast Everett pacific hotel. On the other hand, he is working tirelessly the best he can to get people to support his vision for ministry in the streets of Everett. He doesn't have a lot of the typical credentials, such as a college degree, a big congregation or a large building. But those points don't seem to deter Hampton, a big, energetic man. "God does provide," says Hampton, who isn't too bashful to ask. "You live by faith," says Hampton, who is quick to rattle off story after story about how God has answered the needs of his family and his ministry through the generosity of others. A month's rent for the hotel, income for his family, resources for ministry, even the donation of that bus - they all serve as evidence of god's providence.

"Every year we've been in the ministry, God has put a ram in the Bush," he says, referring to the Old Testament story of how God supplied a ram at the last minute, so Abraham would not have to sacrifice his son. Over the past 18 months though, those Rams have had to cover more than physical needs for Hampton, his wife Julia 29, and their four children. There has been an encounter with racial harassment; 3 deaths in the family including a son; And an arson fire that hit a church in which Mr. Hampton previously served as an evangelist. Most recently, there was a trial of a different sort; criticism over speaking against homosexuality and abortion during a January 15th assembly honoring Martin Luther King junior at Mariner

High School. But for Hampton, a 1982 graduate of Lynnwood High School, each hardship supplies the impetus for building a new "work" for God. Take the incident of racial harassment. In late July 1991, Hampton and his son, Raymond 4th, were outside in a store when Hampton said a man approached them and made repeated racial slurs and threats against the pair. "It could have been someone else's kid," he says of the incident, which he says calls him to think more of teens who make their way alone on the streets of Everett. At that time, Hampton was working in inner-city Seattle with Powerhouse Ministries, where he was licensed as a minister in the Church of God in Christ. He decided to leave that ministry and become a street preacher in Everett, becoming something of a fixture along Colby and Hewitt avenues. Then, a year ago this month came the death of 5-month-old Isaiah. Born with Down syndrome, Isaiah died in his sleep one night at home following a hospital stay with pneumonia. "We woke up and he was gone," Mrs. Hampton, reflecting on the anniversary of their loss. "In the last month I've cried a lot." The tears go for more than Isaiah. Within three months of his death, Mrs. Hampton lost both her mother and her brother. Still, she sees God's hand at work, in this case making her more sympathetic to others who have suffered similar kinds of loss. "He's used the situation we saw as bad and brought a lot of good out of it," says Mrs. Hampton, a 1981 graduate of Everett High School who juggles her time between helping at church, volunteers as an adviser for the African American Student Association at Edmonds Community College's Multicultural Center and taking care of their four children: Trenecsia,9, Raymond IV, 6, Michael, 4, and Catrena, 2. As the Hamptons reckoned with their grief, Mr. Hampton continued with his street preaching, sometimes venturing to the corner of 44th and 196th in Lynnwood. During one of those Lynnwood stops, a motorist stopped and asked Hampton to visit Living Waters Christian Church a new congregation in South County. Hampton eventually joined the congregation staff as an evangelist. In early October, when head Pastor David White was away, an arson fire destroyed a meeting hall that the church was refurbishing. Hampton continued to help the church as it regained its footing, but he says he again felt a call to move on. "The Lord kept dealing with me about starting my own church," he says, leading him to launch Safe in His Arms in November. Several months later, Hampton thrust himself back into the news with his comments about homosexuality and abortion at the high school rally. Mr. Hampton sees no comparison between racial prejudice and speaking against homosexuality, noting the various biblical injunctions against homosexual behavior. "I don't have a phobia," he says. "you don't hate the person; you hate the sin." Hampton also says he has received encouragement from others in the community after the incident reinforcing what he believed is his responsibility to speak the truth as he sees it no matter what. "I'm not going to water it down for anybody," he says. "I'll stand on what I say." Hampton, who is not reticent to talk with media, denies that he is trying to grab headlines. He sees himself as an independent person with a vision that doesn't always mesh with the established ways of doing things. "Everett was not ready for the ministry I was doing as a street preacher," he says. "One church told me they don't want any street people coming into the church." Rather than alter his ministry, Hampton says he'll forge his own path for now. "People have been serving the church," he says. "It's time for the church to be serving the people." Hampton believes his new church though small, is a place where anyone, even the most down and out can feel welcome. "We've got a black preacher with a (mostly) white congregation," he says. That way you know God's in it. "Hampton also longs to see growth in his street ministry which he now calls Street Outreach Services (SOS), he longed for a building in Everett that his church can call it's home. One that can be based of operations for this street. Where the building will come from, he doesn't know same with the money, much less the church members who could make such a place work. But that's fine for Raymond Hampton lll, faith got him this far and faith will see him through to the end. "I can't see it right now he says of the future, but I believe."

The Everett Herald Newspaper

SIDEWALK FOOD BANK DRAWS IRE OF BUSINESS
Downtown businessmen want food bank moved

Rev. Ray Hampton advertise a free food giveaway in the heart of downtown Everett on a recent Friday afternoon. Even though it's something Hampton has been doing off and on for three years nearby business owners were shocked to see scores of people lined up to receive the food donations along the sidewalk in front of Seafirst bank at Hewitt and Colby Bob Wilson brought the matter to the attention of the Everett City Council last week. Wilson passed around a photograph showing the crowd of people gathered on the sidewalk. An armored car, presumably conducting business at the bank was parked at the curb. Wilson said Rev. Hampton's food bank was disruptive to downtown business, and he asked the City Council to do something about it. Police chief Mike Campbell said he has dealt with Rev. Hampton before and thought he had moved his ministry to Snohomish. Campbell said he was surprised to learn that Hampton had returned to Everett. Hampton flyer advertised the food giveaway through the Safe in His Arms Christian Center. Wilson said Hampton plans to distribute food every Friday afternoon. Chief Campbell said Hampton like the audience his high-profile food bank attracts. "it's legal. He has a food handler permits, "Campbell said.

Counselor frank Anderson said Hampton should have to get a permit to set up his operation on a city sidewalk. Hampton said lots of people don't like his sidewalk food bank because it draws a crowd of needy people. He said he would like the city to offer him an alternative instead of ordering him to take his food bank somewhere else. "Businessmen downtown want to clean up the city, and so do I Hampton said.

The Everett Herald Newspaper

Chapter 6

SILVER LAKE CHAPEL

1994-1997

February 1994, I was feeling in my spirit that it was time to rise to another level with my passion. On one Sunday evening between 9:30-10:30pm while still living in south Everett, I remember walking around my home and telling my wife, Julia I was feeling like something great was getting ready to happen in our life. As you're reading this, you might be thinking, God is getting ready to do it again! Not that what I was doing was not great, but I knew I felt in my spirit that God was getting ready to expand Ray Hampton Outreach Ministries, but this time He was going to do something that was going to introduce me to another level of ministry. I remember sharing with my wife that if someone calls me tonight and ask me to be their staff evangelist, to help grow the Kingdom of God, as well as their local church; I would say yes. I'm sure there are many times in life where you have felt a tug in your heart or that small voice telling you where to go, what to do and when to do it, but because of your disobedience for not doing what you heard your blessing was delayed and this

137

causes you to take a detour from your destiny. Your disobedience caused you to suffer consequences through life and the people that you were connected to, to go through unnecessary turmoil in their own life. All of that could have been avoided if you just would've been obedient to the calling of God on your life. A lot of times, opportunity is knocking at your door, but if you don't open the door and let opportunity in, you will never experience what it really means to live a life full of passion and purpose. I do realize that every good opportunity might not be a God opportunity because some opportunities can be a distraction as well. But I really want you to be honest with yourself, when an opportunity comes to your life, ask yourself this question, "Am I not taking this opportunity because it's not of God or am I fearful that things might not turn out the way I expected it to be?"

I believe one of the greatest dishonesties is dishonesty within yourself. Dishonesty within yourself is when you know that you are supposed to do something great and have been praying for it to come to pass and when what you been praying for finally arrives you say this is not it, when the truth is it is it. What's happening to you are two things: double-mindedness and fear.". I want you to remember the following acronyms for fear and faith. F.E.A.R. (False Evidence Appearing Real) and F.A.I.T.H. (Forsaking All I Trust Him). Therefore, it is so important to keep the faith that you started with because it will be the same faith that you will end with. A very important reminder to yourself is that you did not promote yourself, your promotion was given to you from God, so accept it and don't reject it. God has always provided everything that was needed for Ray Hampton Outreach Ministry. Like I said earlier in the chapters, "if it's His WILL all God needed was a Ray" and wherever there is a "Will (Gods will) there will be a Ray (Gods Way)! Remember that Sunday evening? How I was walking around my home on a Sunday evening between 9:30-10:30pm? Well, guess what happened? I did receive that phone call and it was amazing! That evening when the phone rang it was just an ordinary ring like any other ring, but on the other end of the line was a Pastor whose name was Dave Anderson, an associate pastor of a local church in South Everett called Silver Lake Chapel which was known as a mega church of about a minimum of 1800 people. The pastor began to share with me how their staff had been reading all the newspaper articles in the Everett Herald and Seattle Times about the feeding of the hungry, homeless, and helpless children, youth and adults that were living on the streets, the giving away of hundreds of turkeys on the streets, the blankets, clothing and so much more. He proceeded to share that I should come out and visit one of their services. WOW! Don't tell me that God will not do it! I'm just going say this now, WON'T HE DO IT? I immediately started to get that same feeling as when I was playing the bass guitar back in 1989 at the Powerhouse Church of God in Christ with Eric Jenkins on that Hammond B3 organ as the drums were beating on two and four, the people (saints) of God jumping and dancing (shouting) around the church, skipping and leaping and jumping. Remember, I shared with you about Elder Craig Jackson; the man who jumped so high he almost jumped through the ceiling. Well, when I received the phone call, another song started ringing in my spirit; CAN'T NOBODY DO YOU LIKE JESUS, CAN'T NOBODY DO YOU LIKE THE LORD, CAN'T NOBODY DO YOU LIKE JESUS BECAUSE HE'S, MY FRIEND! HE PICKED ME UP AND....... (Okay let me stop right here because, I'm getting happy and excited all over again the same way I felt in 1994 as I'm writing my story, JESUS!)

That following Sunday night I got in my car so quick I felt like," Bat man and Robin" and once I was in the car I turned into a "speed racer". If you're wondering what "Bat Man and Robin" and "Speed Racer" is and what it has to do with Sunday night. They were cartoons and they both moved quickly when it came speed. I finally arrived at the church at 5:00pm for the 6:00pm service. I arrived an hour early at Silver Lake Chapel, so I wouldn't be late for service, Praise the Lord! When I got out of my automobile and started to walk toward the building, my legs start to shake like Elvis Presley, my feet started to move like James Brown and once I arrived at the

Foyer of the church, I did the Sammy Davis Jr. and ended up doing the Michael Jackson moon walk all the way to the pew where I would sit. Many thoughts were going through my head, such as "Was this the moment I had been praying for?"

I was sitting on the far back pew, halfway through the praise and worship service, an usher whose name is Dave Stout began to come towards my way. Because I'm so used to preaching on the streets I began to think, "Why is he looking at me that way, he doesn't know me like that." If you're from the inner-city you understand the preceding phrase. But with a quickness I realized that he didn't know me, he was asked to come to the back seat and escort me to the front seat. With over eight-hundred people attending the night 6:00pm service that evening, I was wondering how the pastors knew that I was even in the building, then I finally figured it out, not only have they seen my face through the media multiple times, but I was also one of five people of color in the whole building. So, I guess that made it easy to recognize me.

As I walked to the front of the church going to the seat, the usher continued to guide me and escort me to the platform to sit with the pastors. As I scanned across the sanctuary, I will never forget the thought that came to mind, which was all my needs were getting ready to be met. When the praise and worship service was over and the announcements had been read, the senior pastor introduced me to the congregation as his special guest, he called me "The Street Evangelist." After sharing with the congregation the feeding of the hungry, homeless, and helpless in downtown Everett, the church began to stand up, clap and cheer. The place exploded with praise and thanksgiving. While the cheering and applauding was getting louder and louder, Pastor Vince Schott shouted over the microphone and said, "Everyone come give my brother, the Street Evangelist, a whole lot of money." And then I jumped up out of my seat with a quickness and shouted to everyone as well and said, "Do what your Pastor told you to do (Just Joking)." People came from everywhere. Young, old, white, brown and black (well at least the four African Americans that were there in attendance.) Pastor Vince had the same usher escort me down the stairs of the platform and asked me to stand there. Once I was in place, he asked the congregation to "come bless my brother the "Street Evangelist." I remember thinking to myself, "Get up, what's taking ya'll so long, Pastor Vince asked you to bless me, start blessing me (Joking......Kinda)." The congregation began to stuff lots of money, and I mean a lot of money in every pocket I had. It was one of the quietest offerings that I've ever seen and been a part of because, remember, I was from the Pentecostal Church; The Church of God in Christ and the offerings were not as quiet; they were louder not because of the music, but because of the coins that dropped in the bucket. This church was a little different, it was a lot of paper money and believe me when I say it was a quiet offering; it really was.

There were hundreds of people that began to give me a hug and great words of encouragement to keep up the great work as they continued to put a lot of money into my pockets. There was so much money in my pockets it began to overflow out, my hands were so filled that I could not even close them; it was so life fulfilling I didn't want it to stop! When all the hugs, words of encouragement and giving was over, I just stood there for a moment like the Statue of Liberty or like I was the Heisman candidate winner in the Heisman pause. After all I was from the Church of God in Christ, and I was used to a second or even sometime a third offering. I shouted out to the congregation with a loud voice like John the Baptist, "what's up, is everyone tired of giving? I asked the usher to quickly hand me a micro phone and the sound man to turn up the sound. Before the people left the sanctuary, I began to sing the first song that came to my spirit as loud as I could. "YOU CAN'T BEAT GODS' GIVING NO MATTER HOW HARD YOU TRY, THE MORE YOU GIVE THE MORE He'll GIVE TO YOU, JUST KEEP ON GIVING..." When that song didn't work, I began to sing another song to the congregation, "NO NO I'M NOT TIRED NO NO I'M NOT TIRED YET (Okay I'm Joking, but I'm so serious). Don't laugh! Do you remember this song from when you were in the store front church? This was the theme song during offering time. That was only the first round there should be at least one more round of giving, but to my knowledge it was over. As the service was dismissed, I was told by one of the ushers that Pastor Vince wanted to speak to me.

I remember replying to him that I would be there after I leave the restroom. The truth is I wanted to go organize and count all the money that I had been blessed with. So, believe me I walked very slowly toward the men's restroom squeezing all my pockets, because I didn't want to lose any money. When I entered the restroom, I went to the nearest stall and gently shut the door with my elbows. I began to remove money from one pocket at a time slowly, so I could organize and count all the money. I remember one of the paper bills falling out of my hands and on its way into the toilet. Like a slow-motion picture, with a quickness I snatched it in midair quicker and better than Wilt Chamberlain, Bill Russell, Kareem Abdul-Jabbar, Moses Malone, Karl Malone, Tim Duncan, Kevin Garnett, Dwight Howard, or LeBron James and said, "No, you don't!" You must speak to your money and tell it what to do or it might do what it wants to do. I know it's called currency, but one thing for sure it wasn't going to flow from me that day!

Once I was finished counting, Are you ready for this? I had over $1600 total, this wasn't monopoly money, but real cash. Talking about excelling in life, I was gliding Like a 747!

There are times in life that you have to stop chasing money, dreams and ideas and realize that money, dreams, and ideas are chasing you. You need to reverse the direction of your thinking process and know without a shadow of doubt that God has your best interest in mind. There are things in life that are not meant for everyone to have and does not belong to them, but when you are obedient to your call and confident, with no insecurities, the thing you were chasing is going to start chasing you. If it is for you and what God has for you it is for you! The reason why I was so excited about the money is because, after two and a half years of reaching out to people on the streets. Even though God has always supplied all my needs for the Ray Hampton Outreach Ministries up to this point in my ministry there had only been one other church that had contributed financially to the ministry. Mill Creek foursquare church pastored by Bob Hasty was a tremendous blessing, after hearing about the amount of people that was being served in the downtown streets of Everett and reading multiple news articles, I received a phone call and he asked me the following question, "What type of P.A. system are you using to talk to the people?" My response was "a megaphone". A few days later, I received a phone call from pastor Bob hasty who had purchased a fully equipped portable P.A. system with microphones and all accessories and donated to the ministry. Pastor Bob Hasty words to me were "to continue reaching people for the Gospel." After leaving the bathroom, I started to walk to the pastors' office for a meeting. When I arrived at the office, I began to share with Pastor Vince and his staff how grateful I was for their financial generosity and hospitality. For the next few hours, we continued in conversations and building relationships. As the evening ended, Pastor Vince said, "Well, let's pray for my brother, the street evangelist as he leaves and let's continue to pray and see what the Lord is up to." Maybe Pastor Vince and his pastoral staff didn't know what God was up to, but I knew what God was up to. After what just happened to me that evening at Silver Lake Chapel, I knew that God was up to something. I quite didn't know what, but I was just waiting for them to hear what God was saying. To be honest with you, I was ready to run back into the sanctuary and repeat the service we had just had. Remember, my background is the Church of God in Christ and I don't know if they knew what a shut-in was, but Ray Hampton was ready to have an all-night shut-in and go back in the sanctuary to previous spot I had just left a few hours before. Yes, you're right, in the front of the Church. All I can think about was the words of a song, "YOU MAY NOT KNOW HOW, YOU MAY NOT KNOW WHEN, BUT HE'LL DO IT AGAIN!

As I left the parking lot of Silver Lake Chapel to go home, I became very anxious and excited about explaining to my wife what had just happened. I'm surprised I did not get a speeding ticket enroute to my home; it was like angels lifted the automobile and placed it in the driveway of my home. The truth is, the angels probably were around my automobile protecting me while I was speeding to get home. Now, before you judge me, I'm sure you have gone over the speed limit once or twice in your own life, so before you point the finger at me, I want you to look down at that big thumb pointing back at you. Have you ever received something in your life, and you were so excited about it that you did not know where to even begin to talk about it? That's how I felt. So, I just began to explain to my wife, Julia when I arrived home about how good God is. The reason I was so excited about the money was because from 1991 until that moment I was receiving $200.00 a week as church evangelist for "Living Waters Church" as well as receiving state assistance, but now the struggle was coming to an end. As I shared with Julia how the night went, she was so excited about the story that her face was glowing with amazement. I mean, she had this look like "thank God for your blessings."

As the week went on, it could not had moved fast enough because I wanted to go back to that church and show my appreciation of thanks. Now, as you read this story, I know you probably are saying right about now, that I just wanted some more money and I have to be honest with you, I really did want to go back and say thank you, but at the same time a little more

147

money wouldn't be a bad idea or at least the congregation can round it off to $2,000 Don't Judge me! As I arrived at the 6:00pm Sunday night service and walked into the sanctuary I was immediately greeted by one of the ushers and escorted into the sanctuary and to the front row. I remember thinking, oh boy I'm about to be a millionaire tonight. Okay, maybe a thousand Aire. Either way, I was there to say thank you after service to the Pastor Vince, his Pastoral team and the congregation. But wait a minute, as I was sitting there on the front row, the Pastor Vince recognizes me and the first sentence that came out of his mouth was, "My brother, the street Evangelist is here tonight again, and the Lord has said to financially bless him again." This time I was prepared with a bucket, money bag and deposit slip – I'm joking! The pastor proceeded by telling me to come to the front of the altar and stand there and I remember thinking to myself, "Master, your wish is my command." Now, before you criticize me, what would you had done if someone called you upfront after they had just given you over $1600 the week before? That's what I thought! Not only did I go up front, but the usher also even walked up and gave me a bucket. I gave the bucket back to him and said, "Why would you give me an offering bucket so small; I asked him to go outside and roll in a dumpster" (Joking... but that's how I felt)

Now, that money bag and deposit slip would have been very useful about now. As I stood there the pastor told everyone to immediately get up and pull some money out of their pockets and drop it into the bucket, but make sure it is a quiet offering. In other words, he wanted them to only put paper bills and checks in the bucket. This would have been a great time for me to have a wireless credit card machine. Sorry, I know, just pray for me! As the offering came to an end, it was all given to me in the sum of almost $1000, I was wondering why this time it was so low, but then realized it was fourth Sunday, the end of the month! (I wish it would've been a 5th Sunday month and maybe there wouldn't had been an issue with the amount, anyway, I'm just kidding)

As the night went on, the pastor wanted to meet with me immediately after service to talk about coming to Silver Lake Chapel to be the church evangelist which was a full-time staff position. As I entertained the conversation with him, I could not believe that this was happening to me, but it was. For a moment, I felt like slapping myself or pouring cold water on my face to wake myself up. But it was not a dream. It was a reality. I'm sure that at once upon a time that you have found yourself in a conversation that did not seem real, but it was. There are times in your life that you will be in a conversation that you have seen yourself in before. Once you engage it, don't leave it just stay engaged because it is what you have been praying for. Now, as Pastor Vince continued to speak, he began to ask me if I would like to go on a tour of the church. What do you think my response was? You are exactly right, YES!

As we were going on the tour, he began to offer me the position of "church evangelist" if I wanted it. In the process of the tour, first my own office was offered, and that was a definite upgrade from a dining room table, second, a secretary that would type and answer all my phone calls, no more voice changes when answering my phone, I was running out of different sounds anyway!

That meant no more handwritten letters; I could not type anyway! And thirty years later, I still don't know how to type, but I do have the fastest three fingers that you have ever seen on a laptop. Oh yeah, and for the phone calls, I no longer have to be the man of many voices even though my secretary voice was awesome because you were guaranteed a phone call back and speaking dates guaranteed, and I never miss an appointment. You understand what was happening? After all this I was offered a monthly salary of $4500.00 with full medical benefits and a three-bedroom home to live in which was over and above my salary. This was all part of my financial package.

The miraculous thing about this is the place where my family and I were currently living was up for sale and we only had a few months left before we had to move. I really want to encourage you that if you ever come up against something that is bigger than you, just know that God has your back.

I really do not know if I was born in the daytime or nighttime, but if it was at night, it sure wasn't last night, but one thing, I knew for sure was that $4500.00 a month was very acceptable. I can now relate to how Warren Buffet or Bill Gates felt when they received an offer!

SILVER LAKE CHAPEL STREET MINISTRY

One of the most committed if not the most committed person that served on the street ministry team at Silverlake chapel was a man named Eugene Hubacek, he was an amazing individual. Even though Eugene was about 13 years older than me, he will always show up every Friday to pack his truck with the items needed to feed the hungry on the streets of downtown Everett. I remember that we will stop by Royal fork buffet on Broadway because they always donated hot chocolate to fill our ten-gallon container every Friday throughout the winter to provide hot drinks for thirsty homeless people that were living on the streets. We would also go by Gai's Bakery to pick up donated pastries and bread to fix Bologna sandwiches; all the food was served off a card table to hundreds of people who called the streets their home, it was to me a city within a city.

SILVER LAKE CHAPEL FOOD BANK
"Compassion Storehouse"

After seeing the need of people within and outside the church that needed food for their families, I decided to approach Pastor Vince about starting a food bank at the church and with no hesitation the answer was yes. After receiving permission, the pastoral team immediately started seeking God through prayer for a location throughout the church that will be big enough to store the nonperishable and perishable food items. Finally, after weeks of prayer, a location was found, it was a storeroom located at what was known as Sather Hall. Sather Hall was a multi-purpose room that was used for many church gathering especially for the high school youth group of over two-hundred and twenty-five youths led by Pastor Brice Greathouse. Sather Hall was what we needed to build a first-class food bank. After surveying this big storeroom as a pastoral team, we decided that only half of the room would be needed for the food bank. Now that the location had been established, it was now time to go to work. There was a team of men that was led by Anton Boggio, who owned a drywall company and a member of the church started to strategize with me on the construction for the food bank. Within two weeks walls, shelves were completely built and it was now time to put a name to it. The first step was to put a name to it, the name "Compassion Storehouse" dropped in my spirit, the second step was the collection of the food items that would be needed to fill the many bags to be provided to individuals and families coming for food on a weekly and or monthly basis. It was now time for the third step which was to ask the congregation to bring the food items. To my amazement, in less than one month the food bank was filled and overflowing, even the refrigerators and freezers were purchased with money that was given through the offering. God was providing not just the need, but had also put His stamp of approval on the food bank. Fourth step was to empower and equip the "Storehouse" food bank team of Silverlake Chapel, so that meant I had to start praying for people that had not just a purpose, but a passion to serve others like they would want to be served. When the announcement was made, "looking for volunteers to help serve in the church food bank." There were two members of the church that came to me and said that they wanted to help in any way they could. Jeanette Wilde and Bea Silva were a tremendous help and excellent team members to the point that they pretty much ran the food bank every week themselves; all I had to do was oversee the ministry. Jeanette and Bea always made sure that the food bank was stocked, so we would never run out of food and scheduling the team of volunteers to serve. Within six months, we grew from serving a handful of people to over 2,000 people a month from nine to eleven every Friday morning. Compassion Storehouse was a tremendous blessing to thousands of people that probably would not have had complete meals for breakfast, lunch, and dinner.

PASTOR BELIEVES IN GOOD WORK, BUT NOT IN JUDGING THOSE IN NEED

Pastor Ray Hampton tells the story about a woman who came to Silver Lake Chapel food bank for help. She was driving a shiny new car. When food bank workers saw her drive up, they came to Hampton to question whether she really was in need. "The Bible says judge not, for you will be judged," Hampton says, he told them. The woman was given food. "Today, she sends us money monthly, "Hampton says. "To judge her, I would have missed a blessing." Like that woman, who had recently lost her job, many come to food banks in expensive vehicles or wearing nice clothes," he says. "Situations change," Hampton says, "and people often have possessions from when they were doing well. "Hampton has helped feed people from all walks of life", from workers laid off by Boeing to alienated youth on the streets of Everett. The pastor of evangelism works under senior pastor Vince Schott Silver Lake Chapel, heading up the southeast Everett churches' food bank. Hampton is also involved in a street ministry that gives out hot dogs, hot cider, cocoa, and coffee each Friday evening on the corner of Wetmore and Hewitt avenues in downtown Everett. "It's Street kids, drug addicts, prostitutes, older people and families with children, too," Hampton says of those served by the street program. With winter chills making streets even meaner, he's collecting coats, shoes, and blankets to share. Administrator Gene Hubacek and ministry helpers assist in the program as part of the Chapel outreach. Hampton also takes the street mission to Seattle pioneer square. A powerfully built man of 32, Hampton values his own family life. He and his wife, Julia both Snohomish County natives, have been married 14 years and have four children. And he is disturbed by behaviors he sees among those he calls "the hopeless, the helpless and homeless." He'll like them to turn away from drugs prostitution and despair. He'll like them to take his Christian message to heart, but First things first. "It's a lot easier to have people listen to you when their stomachs are full," Hampton says. It was the street ministry that brought him to Silver Lake Chapel. In 1992, he started a church in Everett called Safe in His Arms Christian Center, and was feeding the hungry at a busy downtown intersection. "In April 94, I got a call on a Sunday night from Pastor Vince Schott, who said that an associate pastor had read about the work I was doing in downtown Everett." Hampton says he was hired, and since 1994 has helped the Silver Lake Chapel food bank grow from serving about 15 people a month to serving hundreds. With food bank coordinator Bea Silva, Hampton and a staff of workers and volunteers gather food from grocery stores, donated money and going door to door. Thanks to those who donate, about 500 families will enjoy holiday turkeys on Thursday. "70% of the food bank workers once came to us for help," Hampton says now they're on the giving end. "That's when you know you're making a difference."

The Everett Herald News Paper

HOLLYWOOD, CALIFORNIA
Silver Lake Chapel "Evangelism Missions Trip"

July 1994, I went on my first missions training trip to the "Oasis" in Hollywood California. The team was led by Pastor John Serio who was the Junior High youth pastor of the church. We were all headed to California to learn how to do effective witnessing on the street. The Executive Directors Ron & Judy Radachy have been in Hollywood California for over 20 years and has been committed to training teams from all over the United States in evangelism. The teams came from different churches throughout the summer for one week at a time for Evangelism training. This was my first time; I had never been involved in a ministry training school that offered intense learning for one week from morning to evening. There was workshop training in the day and Street witnessing at night. In the evening, we would all get on a big yellow 40 passenger bus to be dropped off at different locations throughout the city for four hours and equipped with ministry tracts for witnessing. As each team was dropped off at their designated

156

locations, Ron who was the bus driver always reminded every team that the bus would arrive back at a certain time for pick up and that it was important for each team to be on time at the pickup location. I remember that his favorite saying was "Be there or cab fare." The team that I was on, was dropped off on Hollywood Boulevard. This was my first time in Hollywood, California and what I had seen on TV and what I was actually seeing now was different, in other words there was more behind the "Hollywood Sign" that was often shown on television.

In about a five block radius there were things like the Chinese theater, stars on the sidewalks with names of well-known actors engraved in gold lettering, very expensive cars and limousines driving up and down the street and a variety of high profile actors and actresses, but what I didn't know is that many street children, teenagers and adults were living on the streets of Hollywood Boulevard in the midst of such high entertainment, expensive vehicles driving up and down the street. It did not take long before I was witnessing to punk rockers, gang members, run away children from their homes, pimps, prostitutes, gay lifestyle, alcoholics, drug addicts, tourist and entertainers and yes, "all this were done in the view of the great Hollywood sign." One major thing that stood out in our training classes was the way we were taught to minister on the streets. Laying hands on someone with-in the church walls is different from laying hands on someone outside the church. You might want to ask for their permission, so they don't think you are trying to hit them. "People that are homeless are always in survival mode." Evidently, one of the young men that was from Texas must had fallen asleep during this part of the teaching because as we were witnessing one night, he decided that he was going to lay hands on this man to pray against the man's will; the man had already said "no thank you," but the young man decided that he was going to do it anyway regardless of what the man had told him. "He said don't touch me," he could've easily just prayed for the man out of respect without laying hands on him, but he decided he wanted to do it his way. He figured that he would do it the way he has always done it in church, he's going to do it the same way on the streets. As he pulled his hand out of his pocket to touch the man, the man pulled out a BIG knife and started to swing at him. The young man from Texas was so scared, he took off and ran, barely getting away from the knife and putting his team members in danger as well. One thing is for sure, I bet he will stay up and won't fall asleep in the next training class and pay close attention. As for me, Raymond Hampton, I don't need a class. In my family we were taught if someone says "don't touch me," "don't touch him." If they say "don't look at me," "don't look at me," and if they ever show you any type of weapon especially a big knife, take off and run as fast as you can.

AFRICA

Nairobi, Kenya

In July 1995, Silver Lake Chapel had a guest speaker named Thomas Muthea who was a Pastor from Kenya in Africa. Pastor Muthea was responsible for multiple churches throughout Africa and a missionary to the United States. As he was speaking during the Sunday services, I began to feel a tug in my spirit pulling me toward Africa. Throughout the service this pull was increasing stronger and stronger. When the service ended, I found myself sitting in the office having a conversation with Pastor Muthea about coming to Africa for a 17-day crusade. Once the date was set, I only had two months to get multiple shots and raise seventeen hundred dollars for a round trip ticket. Just a side note; "It was definitely going to be a round trip!" I always lived by certain mottos throughout the last 30 plus years of doing outreach ministry, such as; "Wherever God guides He provides" or "If it's Gods will, it's Gods bill," On the next Sunday, Pastor Vince announced to the church with great excitement in his voice "Our church evangelist, Pastor Ray Hampton will be going to Africa in two months to preach the gospel." As the service continued, I remember sitting in my seat and saying to myself, "What just happened?" Immediately service was over, hundreds of people were either calling my office phone, greeting me in the parking lot or throughout the building saying how excited they were for me to have such a great opportunity. Not only was my Church family excited for me, which was great, but ultimately what sealed it was that my wife, Julia was in full support of me going which meant a lot because from the beginning she had been and always will be my number one supporter. The scriptural text in the bible says,

> *"He who finds a wife finds a good thing and obtains favor from the Lord."*

Proverbs 18:22 ESV

For years, I have always known that my favor and blessings from God for my life for outreach came with a connection of having a "Praying and committed" wife. I personally believe I have favor from God. My Children who were in elementary and middle school were just as excited as everyone else; to all of them it was just a WOW factor. My dad and mom were calling every family member and friends in St. Louis, Mo. and throughout the state of Washington to let them know what was going on in my life. Besides my wife, my mom was also my cheerleader at another level; everything that I did in the ministry of outreach, and I mean everything, she promoted all of it by the way of telephone. If you have ever

160

met my mom, you would never forget her, she would always share information with you with a kind spirit and would give you more than what was needed. In her own words, her excitement for me; "My oldest son Ray Ray who was born in Hawaii when my husband was serving oversees in Vietnam, you know he is a minister and have been feeding the people on the streets for years in downtown Everett, you know he preaches at that big church. Anyway, he is going to Africa. Okay bye. I got to make some more phone calls before it gets too late, I'll talk to you later...alright bye." (My MOM was a great lady who loved her children and was very supportive (1946-2010). I Remember how I shared with you earlier in the text, "Wherever God guides He provides," that is exactly what happened. On a Wednesday night after service, I was approached by Louis Bremond who was one of our members at the church. Louis stated to me that he wanted to donate toward my Africa trip and that he had a huge bottle/Jar full of coins and that he was going to bring it to church and give it to me and whatever the amount is when counted, he will double it. After a week had gone by, the amount that was counted was $714.00. When I saw Louis the following service and shared what the amount was, I will never forget his response, "That much money was in that glass Jar? Man, okay who do I make the check out to? I'll just round it off to $800.00." His total financial contribution was over $1500.00 dollars.

THANKSGIVING

The next outreach that we started at the Silver Lake Chapel was for Thanksgiving which we titled "Project Box". Project box was such a great food giveaway for the holiday. Many people that gave to the food bank also gave a box filled with holiday food for Thanksgiving. Can you imagine hundreds of people on a Sunday walking through the church doors not just with their Bible in hand, but with little brown boxes filled with all the food that a family would need to have a great Thanksgiving meal. Boxes were filled not only with nonperishable food for holiday, but so many turkeys were given that our freezer in the food bank was overflowing with meat.

CHRISTMAS

Even though these other ministries were exceeding, one of my favorite time of the year was Christmas because I believe that every child on Christmas morning should have a gift under the tree to unwrap. Serving a church of 2300 people every week, I knew that if each person could bring a gift, we would be able to provide two to three-thousand toys for children. My team and I decided to do something in the foyer and set up a huge giving tree were every time a person entered or exited the church, all they had to do was pull the tag off of the giving tree and bring back a gift for the child's age or sex, during the week or whenever they arrived at the next church service. I remember walking into the sanctuary one Sunday morning for the 8:00am service and was so excited to see a tree full of tags that represented many boys and girls that would be receiving toys. After the third service which started at 11:15am and ended around 1:00pm, I walked out of the sanctuary and saw an empty tree with no tags. I was so excited that so many people decided to get involved. That following week we had to refill the tree with more tags and again the following week the tree was empty after the last service. Finally, the day came when it was time to give out the toys and as you probably already imagined, many children were blessed that Christmas of 1995. The beginning of 1996 started out as a big year. In February, I attended Christian Faith Center Internationals' Vision Conference where Casey Treat is the Pastor, one of his guest speakers was Tim Storey from Los Angeles, California. This was my first time seeing him. I was first amazed by how young he was as he was getting ready to speak to thousands that were attending the vision conference. Within five minutes of Tim speaking, the church exploded with people worshiping God and Tim running around the sanctuary praying for people as they were falling out throughout the sanctuary. Two months later, at the end of April, I was doing my first evangelism conference titled "Evangelism Explosion" in front of a packed house. I remember when Tim arrived at the church, he had a national recording artist with him named Tim Miner who is an incredible singer. After service was over, we all went out to dinner for fellowship and to exchange contact information and for the next two years I was attending a celebrity bible study once a month in Hollywood, California that was started by Diane Canon and Tim. Month after month, I was sitting by actors and actresses that were on local TV daily and weekly.

Within the first year, I was sitting in my office one evening when I received a phone call from Tommy Barnett, the pastor of Phoenix First Assembly of God church in Phoenix, Arizona. He had received one of my books titled "Building Leaders for Evangelism "from Tim Storey at an airport and wanted to talk to me about the Los Angeles International Church, which had recently purchased a historical hospital in the Los Angeles area. As I was sitting in my office, I began to wonder who was Tommy Barnett because I had never heard of him. I just figured it was another pastor who had a dream, not that having a dream is bad, I was busy dreaming myself, so I just threw his contact information into my round file, better known as a garbage can. As I left my office later on that evening, I decided to stop by Family Christian Bookstore to look for some evangelism material and as I was looking around the store, I noticed a book that sat on the shelf titled, "Is There a Miracle in your House" by Tommy Barnett. I immediately began to wonder if this was the same person that contacted me by phone regarding the Los Angeles

International Church. I took the book off the shelf and read the biography and to my amazement, it was the same person. I immediately ran out of the bible bookstore and unlocked my car, jumped into my seat, started my car did a couple of donuts in the parking lot and burnt some rubber off my tires as I took off out of the driveway. As I'm writing this book, I just had a thought, 30 years later. I hope the store management didn't think I was stealing anything. As I started my car and headed back to the church, I kept hoping that the custodian hadn't emptied the round file (garbage can) yet. Once I arrived at the church, I ran hundred-yard sprint straight to my office and to the round fie (garbage can), and guess what? WOW... I never thought I would be so excited about seeing garbage in a garbage can. It was no longer garbage to me; it was a million-dollar piece of paper with Pastor Tommy Barnett's phone number on it. Time could not go fast enough throughout the night before it was time to go to the office where I will be able to call Pastor Tommy. When I called the church, I left a message and even received a phone call, not by him, but his son Pastor Matthew Barnett of the LA International Church. For the next two years, I traveled faithfully every month to Los Angeles, California to attend the war room meetings that were hosted weekly on Television Trinity Broadcasting Network.

Chapter 7

THE SEATTLE INTERNATIONAL CHURCH AND DREAM CENTER

1997-2001

After serving as Evangelism Pastor at Silver Lake Chapel from 1994 (January) -1997 (April), it was finally time for me to move to the next season of my life. After much prayer, fasting and a consistent tugging of my heart for something more, it was time to move on. Pastor Vince had made the announcement to the congregation that "Pastor Ray and his family will be moving on, to pursue the calling of God, their life in the ministry of evangelism." When the announcement was made, there were many tears in the building, as well as hand clapping for a great job of serving at the church. Not knowing where we were going to live in few months or where the next cheque was coming from, I relied on the following scripture;

> *¹³ I can do all things [which He has called me to do] through Him who strengthens and empowers me [to fulfill His purpose—I am self-sufficient in Christ's sufficiency; I am ready for anything and equal to anything through Him who infuses me with inner strength and confident peace.*

Philippians 4:13 AMP

Trust in and rely confidently on the LORD with all your heart And do not rely on your own insight or understanding. In all your ways know and acknowledge and recognize Him,_And He will make your paths straight and smooth [removing obstacles that block your way].

Proverbs 3:5-6 AMP

Immediately the church service was over, a couple in the church named Roger & Terry Olson approached me about where my family was going to live, at that moment I had no idea, but GOD DID! Later, my wife and I eventually met with the Olson's' about moving into their home in Lynwood, WA. The date arrived to go look at the house to meet the Olson's, my wife and I were so excited that God was again getting ready to supply another need.

19 And my God will liberally supply (fill until full) your every need according to His riches in glory in Christ Jesus.

Philippians 4:19 AMP

After growing up in Lynnwood from sixth grade until l graduated from Lynnwood high school in 1982, I had a very good landscape of the city, so I knew the area well. Once we arrived at the home, we were so excited because it was not an ordinary home. It was a split level three-bedroom home in a great community. Once we started the meeting, it was not long before Terry Olson said, "if you guys want the house it's yours". I remember thinking "how am I going to pay for this gorgeous home?" As I was thinking, the next statement that

Terry Olson said was a mind shocker. "Roger and I decided to let your family stay in the house until you get established in your ministry, all we ask is that you cover the utilities." All I could say at that moment was, "What a mighty God we serve".

28 And we know [with great confidence] that God [who is deeply concerned about us] causes all things to work together [as a plan] for good for those who love God, to those who are called according to His plan and purpose.

Romans 8:28 AMP

Well, after getting settled in our home, it was now time to move the street ministry from the corner of Colby and Hewitt to pioneer square in downtown Seattle. In the year of 1997, spring and summer had come and gone; it was now time for one of my favorite times of the year, football season.

Since I had two sons, they had to play football or they would not be allowed to play any sports, okay, don't take me seriously, I'm joking, Kinda. Thank God both of my boys were aggressive and love competition. Living in Snohomish County, we had the MTYAA (Mountlake Terrace Youth Athletic Association) which represented young people to play sports. One of the games that we played was against the Brier Bulldogs and my son played for the Mountlake Terrace Trojans and of course, we won the game. As the game was being played, I met one of the parents of a player. Her son, Kyle played for the Bulldogs and as the game was in action, we began to talk about what I do for a living. I shared with her that I was in full time ministry and was in transition; the next words that came out of her mouth were, "You should meet my husband, he is a mortgage broker and works in real estate." "That was music to my ears." After exchanging contact information as soon as we were done demolishing their team and snacks were passed out, I immediately called her husband, Kevin. I remember leaving a voicemail for him to give me a call and later that evening, that call came. I shared with Kevin that I had met his wife and she advised me to call him. Later that week, I went to Bellevue to Kevin's office and shared with him where we were financially in our life and the transition we were in our life. Kevin shared with me that there was a new house located in the city of Lake Forest Park which was the same city where he was currently living, and the house was located next door to his home. Later that week, I had an appointment to go see the home in Lake Forest Park. As I was driving up and down the street looking for the home, all I kept seeing were very nice large square footage two story homes, but in my mind, I was expecting a small rambler or something similar. When I verified the address 4033 NE 197th Street and realized that I was in front of the home, it was not only the biggest home my family had ever lived in, but we were getting ready to be a first-time homeowner. Are you ready for this? December of 1997, my wife and I signed for the home and our family moved in that same month. Merry Christmas to us! We were FIRST TIME HOMEOWNERS!

So many other things happened that month as well, my first cousins Terrance and Tyrrell who were three-year-old twins came to live with us, so now my family had extended from four to six children. As you can see, expansion was all around us (Adopted in 2007).

In the month of June 1998, which was six months later I restarted the Seattle International Church at the Cedar Valley Elementary school gymnasium. All my children were one hundred percent supportive of starting the church (I Think so!). Thank God for their support, but since they were all in elementary school, I guess they really didn't have a choice. For the next six months, my wife and children were such a blessing to this re-reestablished work. I remember everyone loading and unloading the equipment out of the bus Sunday after Sunday, putting mailings together around the dining room table every month. I had made many promises that whoever could get the most envelopes done I would buy them a Slurpee at 7-Eleven or any place they wanted to go. I did this because work had to be done. Now that I look back at that moment, I hope it was bribery or free child labor. It was just children that would rather load equipment into out of busses, buildings, and storages instead of going outside to play with their friends. Isn't God good? Now, if my children were writing this book, I'm absolutely positive that their perspective may be a little different, okay, a whole lot of difference than what you're reading. But since it's my book, this is how I see it, PRAISE THE Lord!

A year and a half later, we signed a lease to meet at the Snohomish County Christian school in June 1998. What an amazing time we had at this location and our ministry was still expanding. Before we arrived at this location, we were always praying for transportation to bring people to church, and would you believe that our prayers were answered in abundance. The school no longer wanted their fleet of buses and offered them to our ministry. Even though it sounded great, in my mind what do you think I was thinking? You're right, how much? The price was absolutely a blessing! Would you believe that we purchased five fifteen passenger and two forty passenger buses for $400.00 each, I know what you are probably thinking by now, did they run? My answer is YES!

FISHING FOR MEN

From Seattle to Everett, Shoreline to Lynnwood, Pastor Ray Hampton takes his ministry to the streets

If it is God's will, it's God's bill. That's how Ray Hampton puts it. And it would be difficult to argue with him. For seven years now, Hampton has been ministering Christianity in the Seattle-Lynnwood-Everett area, giving away clothes and food to the homeless and money to the financially constrained, while at no point having a steady, reliable income of money. But the way Hampton sees it, he's got the most reliable source possible, God. People have got to understand, Hampton says, "you can do ministry, you can enjoy ministry, and you don't have to beg." One would be hard pressed to find another good explanation for the success Hampton has had since July 1991, from his days ministering to the homeless on the street corners in Everett and Seattle (which he still does). Hampton has now planted a church in Lynnwood; Seattle international church, opened on June 7th. Right now, services are held in the gym at Cedar Valley elementary school since the church is currently lacking a permanent site. That's OK with Hampton because to him, the church is more of a stabilizing force. He says his real calling is out on the streets where he looks to "meet every need." you can't say, "honey, I think I'm going to go catch me some catfish today, then sit down all day and watch TV and eat Doritos, waiting for that catfish to come hopping through the door," Hampton says, "it doesn't work that way. We have to get up, leave the four walls of our church and go fishing (for men)." So, every Tuesday night, Hampton works toward his goal of knocking on every door in Lynnwood with his "adopt an apartment" program. He tries to find out how he can meet needs whether it be through helping a resident with his or her electricity bill, giving out clothes or simply brightening up a day with a popsicle.

When he holds a "sidewalk Sunday school" at the complex." "Right here in Lynnwood we have people bleeding eternally; they're crying out for help," Hampton said, "I'm not the physician's assistant. I help 'Dr.' Jesus. He meets that need. He said to me, 'if I'm in it, I'll take care of it.' Now my goal is to find people with problems. A lot of people never go to church. You have to take the church to them." It seems to be working. In less than two months, Hampton has seen his congregation grow from just 30 the first Sunday to 140 on July 25th. "The main purpose for the church is to be a hospital for the sick," said Hampton, speaking metaphorically. "Hospital is for the sick, not the well." And Hampton, a security guard by day at Lynnwood High School has grand plans for how he can reach the "sick" in the Lynnwood area. He wants to find a permanent home for his church in a large facility he will call the "Dreamcenter." He hopes to eventually house a private Christian School, to be directed by his wife, an educator. He also said he wants to be able to have a clothing and food bank open five days a week and serve hot meals three days a week. Hampton says he is close to procuring a facility. As usual, Hampton is believing God for the facility, just as he believed God for the donated bus he uses to get the homeless from Seattle's skid rows to church, for the donated meal wagon he uses to deliver food to the homeless and for the freezer donated by Baskin and Robbins to give kids popsicles. "There really is no set plan," Hampton said. "It's up to the Lord."

The Enterprise Newspaper

A DREAM COME TRUE

Couple turns pawn shop into a ministry for the poor

MOUNTLAKE TERRACE - The Seattle International Dream Center, previously the site of the Mountlake Terrace Loans Pawnshop, opened its doors to a little fanfare, but for Rev. Ray Hampton and his wife, Julia, no ribbon cutting ceremony and champagne was needed. After nine years of hard work, on the part of the couple and the Seattle International Church of Lynnwood, the center is a dream come true. "That was all the celebration necessary," Hampton said. The newly painted storefront houses a food bank, clothing bank and Community Resource Center. It will be a home base for Hamptons' mobile ministry, which delivers home cooked meals, ribs and chicken, potato salad and the word to homeless people in king and Snohomish counties. Pastor Gary Ragsdale, with Everett Word of Truth Christian Center, met Hampton nine years ago, when Hampton was ministering on the streets of Everett. The Dream Center is unique Ragsdale said. "It's a place for people to get better, to hear the gospel, to get them jobs, to meet their total needs," he said.

"Sometimes in a church setting you meet their spiritual needs, but not all the needs they have." The Dream Center is intended for all people of South Snohomish County. Its emphasis is on rekindling the human spirit, especially one that's been trampled by drugs, alcoholism, job loss or life on the streets, Ray Hampton said. "So far, neighbors have welcomed the center." "There's a concern anytime you put a Resource Center that you might draw unwanted people," said Julia Hampton, a former School Teacher. "We understand this is a family-oriented community. We want to make sure there's no one doing any harm. But what you might call unwanted, may not be so." For now, the center offers food, clothing, toys and a service that provides home grocery delivery to elderly or disabled people. But by the end of this month, the Hamptons and a score of volunteers expect to be able to tutor schoolchildren, offer computer training to young and old, and construct job seekers in the basics of filing out a job application. The center's backyard is home of a steel container full of canned goods. The Hamptons plan to add a basketball court and a children's playground. Hundreds of people have donated to the center. Jack Roberts, former owner of Jack Roberts appliance, donated refrigerators, freezers, and office equipments. Church members donated food, clothing and two passenger vans. Students at Lynnwood high school donated more than 900 toys. Hampton began his ministry in 1991 on the street, at the corner of Everett Colby and Hewitt avenues.

Years ago, the Hamptons were struggling to juggle jobs, college, and care for their three children. To make ends meet they stood in line at the food bank. As a result of how they sometimes were treated standing in that line, they vowed to treat others better. "I want to praise people and let them know it takes a lot of dignity to go to a food bank," Julia Hampton said. As a young man, Hampton knew he didn't want to be accepting a handout ever. "For that to change, I knew I had to shift gears, work two jobs instead of one job, get an education, do whatever it takes," he said. "Walk through the doors of the Dream Center, and Ray Hampton is ready to spread the message of hope and to help," said pastor Henry Jenkins, with Seattle Powerhouse Church of God in Christ. "He's got a special touch; he's good people. He's the man of the hour," Jenkins said

The Everett Herald Newspaper

TERRACE CENTER TRIES TO HELP DREAMS

MOUNTLAKE TERRACE - Pastor Ray Hampton is at it again, but this time he has a building here to house the materials he uses to help people in need throughout the Puget

Sound area. "God couldn't have placed me in a better place," Hampton said about his first Dream Center, located on 56th Ave in Montlake Terrace. The center is located in what used to be the Montlake Terrace pawn shop. Montlake Terrace is one of the poorest cities in the county. "They aren't in need of another church, but they are in need of the basics," said Hampton. Seattle International Church congregation meets at the Cedar Valley Elementary School gym in Lynnwood. It now has a Dream Center, a place where anyone can go for free to fulfill their basic needs food, clothing, and a computer Resource Center for youth. His goal, which has been the same since he started his personal mission on a street corner in 1991, is "Find the major need in a community, then fill it." He started the church almost two years ago, he said, "because it's a more effective way of helping people." I wanted to duplicate myself." Hampton said he believes the church is his responsibility to take care of those in need, not the government.

With little money in hand, Hampton tells the story of how God has provided all he has needed to start the first of many Dream Centers and he has plans for Washington. "After the owner of the property knew what our mission was, he basically told me to write my own contract," Hampton said. As for things they have needed to start a food and clothing bank, many local businesses and individuals have donated items to them. Flynn hall of carpet cents, a Lynnwood business, donated carpeting for the building. All of the drywall and remodeling in the building, as well as signs, were donated. Jack Roberts home appliance has donated several items during the last couple years, such as a copy machine and transportation vans for Hampton, which he uses to pick up homelessness and transport them to a restaurant where he feeds them a hot meal weekly. Others too have been so giving, such as a local couple who bought, then donated, two new freezers for the food bank. Hampton, 35, also is a public speaker and author. He is looking forward to the two-year anniversary of the Seattle International Church on June 4th, 5th and sixth. The church will welcome Matthew Barnett, the founder of the first Dream Centers, which are very successful in Southern California. The food and clothing bank, along with a computer Resource Center for youth will open the beginning of August. When it begins, the food bank will be open on Fridays from 9:30 to 11:30 AM; the clothing bank will be open Thursday and Friday mornings and the computer Resource Center will be open after school to youths on Mondays, Wednesdays and Fridays for high school students, and on Tuesdays and Thursdays for middle school. The Resource Center will be run by volunteers who work with computers professionally, he said.

The Enterprise Newspaper

MISSION FIELD IN OUR OWN BACKYARD

"I believe we are flying over the mission field, while trying to get to the mission field," Pastor Ray Hampton stated quietly. "Our mission field now is America." Pastor Hampton is a man of imposing size, with a firm grip that engulfs the hand he greets, and warm, brown eyes that draw you into his story. It is the story of the disadvantage and homeless from Seattle to Everett. In July 1991, Pastor Ray answered the call of the Lord laid on his heart. He went to AA Rentals, rented a megaphone and card table, and moved to the corner of Colby and Hewitt. In the warm summer night, his baritone voice echoed off buildings and cars, as he preached, "for God so loved the world, he gave us only begotten son... come to know Jesus. He wants to meet you." The growing crowd clustered around him. Three hours later, hoarse, but satisfied, he folded the table legs, packed the megaphone, and carried his tools to the car. He was tired, particularly after working all day at Safeway, but excited because he had done what the Lord asked of him. He knew he would return the following Friday night. For two and a half years, Pastor Ray never missed a Friday night on that Everett Street Corner, but after six months he realized, "People needed more than preaching, "said Hampton. He saw hunger in drawing faces. It looked worse in the eyes of people staring

179

back at him, and he realized they wouldn't be leaving this place for warm bed. For many of them, their beds were the cold hard concrete they were standing on.

He saw people huddled together for warmth, as the nights grew cold and winter advanced, he saw shoes with paper stuffed into them for souls and coats resembling rags more than coats. He wept inside. Neighboring businesses donated pastries, donuts, hot dogs, and drinks, which he passed out to cold, grateful hands. He continued to preach, but he also acquired a growing realization that he had to do more. The second year on Colby and Hewitt, his streetside congregation grew to 300, and the police talked to him about him crowding the streets. Thanksgiving that year, Hampton gave away 200 turkeys to the homeless and disadvantage. The line wrapped around the entire block. He remembered a lady who came, her face careworn and wrinkled. Her clothes torn. A stick was rolled into her hair. It was probably the only curler she could afford. Marveling she still cared he asked, "Where do you live, sister?" "In the woods, by the railroad tracks," she replied. Though he never saw her again, he later went to the bridge over to those tracks. With the pole, he dropped down bags of food, watching as the "forgotten" people swarmed to pick them up. In 1995, after fasting and prayer, Hampton said the Lord led him to form Seattle International Church. They meet at 11:00 AM Sundays in the gym at Lynnwood Cedar Valley elementary school. In April 1997, he extended his outreach to the homeless in Seattle. Every Thursday night, using donated buses, drivers from Seattle International Church go to the corner of 2nd and Washington to pick up the homeless. No one advertises this service, except for word of mouth among the street people. Volunteers pick up from 20 to 60 people, sometimes children, and take them to the Powerhouse Church of God in Christ in Seattle. They lend their facility Thursday night to feed the homeless and preach the gospel before taking them back to bridges, or against buildings with cardboard boxes as beds - their home.

Power House Church of God in Christ ordained and licensed Pastor Ray Hampton. Pastor Henry Jenkins, Senior Pastor, is a trusted mentor for Pastor Ray. Hampton dreams of a church facility where he can provide housing and training to the homeless, as well as initiate a food and clothing Bank. "Some food banks are food pantries, not banks," he said, "because they don't know what they have. Like a bank, they can tell you what they have to the penny." Pastor Ray and his family received their last paycheck February 1997 from Silver Lake Chapel church and they have lived by the model "whatever you want in life give it away." "If you need a car, help someone else get a car. Whatever you want in life, you must give it away first," said Hampton. Hampton and his family put feet to Luke 6; 38, "give and it will be given unto you" and as they "give away," the Lord meets every personal need as well as the needs of the ministry, noted Hampton.

Hampton seminary degrees may be absent, but his conviction to be an effective lay minister in the area he feels God has called him is strong. "I have an anointing for the streets. I don't go to school to study to be a pastor, how to reach the homeless or how to show people the love of Christ, but the Lord gave me a passion for it. Theology degrees are wonderful, but I have a B. A given to me by the Lord, it is my "Born Again" degree, and that's what I need to get out of my seat, on to my feet and hit the streets answering the call of my lord."

NORTHWEST NEWS

SEATTLE INTERNATIONAL CHURCH GROWS

"In 1995, I was already doing some street preaching and feeding of homeless people in Seattle, but everyone I met kept telling me I needed to visit Los Angeles to see what was going on at the Dream Center. I finally visited and returned every month for two years to learn more. The Los Angeles Dream Center was instrumental in my vision to start the Seattle International Church where we reached out to the inner-city residents through food and clothing distribution. We are now feeding approximately 200 hungry people a day, and we operate a food bank on Sundays. We have also launched the adopt- a- block ministry which I learned about through Los Angeles International church. On Saturdays, we send out a swat team into the community - SWAT stands for Soul Winning Across Town. We began our church with 38 people and the ministry has grown to 130 people in one year 95% of which are new believers."

Dream Center Today

L.A. International Church

Chapter 8

THE MOVE TO CITY CHURCH

2002-2003

It even gets better, in 2002 there was a young girl who was four years old named Brittany attending The City Church. As foster parents for many years we always had an open door for any child that needed short- or long-term care. My wife, Julia was introduced to her, as she was in foster care. Brittany and her foster mother both attended The City Church. My wife and I eventually introduced Brittany to our family. A teacher at Lake Forest Park Elementary School where our children attended, also brought to my wife's attention about a little girl that needed placement. A few months later, Brittany was introduced to our family (children). Even though it was an adjustment for our family after much prayer we started the process of adopting Brittany to be part of our family. We were also blessed to have Brittany's mother in our lives as well. We were able to cultivate a relationship with her birth family as well as her paternal grandmother.

After multiple meetings, Brittany finally came to live with us and now our family expanded to seven children (adopted in

2007). The amazing thing regarding Brittany is that the Church that we were attending that year was, The City Church in Kirkland Washington Pastored by Wendell Smith. Without even knowing it, Brittany was attending The City Church as well with her current foster mother. What is so amazing about this story is that Brittany's last name is, are you ready for this? You got it "Hampton", so it was definitely meant to be. Guess what Brittany's last name is after we adopted Her? You got it "Hampton". If you haven't figured it out what's is going, let me help you. Brittany had the same last name as our family. God had a plan!

In October of 2002, I attended a Vision Conference in Kirkland, Washington at The City Church. The guest speaker that night was Pastor Tommy Barnett from Phoenix First Assembly of God Church in Phoenix, Arizona. As I began to listen to his message, there were things stirring up in my spirit on how to reach people more effectively. I was already connected in ministry because of the previous years as you already have read in earlier chapters. Just in case you forgot, remember the phone call I received and threw the information in the round file (Garbage Can) and went back to retain it? You got it! It's the same person from the L.A. International Church and The L. A. International Dream Center. As I was leaving out of the church after service, I was approached by Pastor Aaron Haskins, the City Networking Pastor. Pastor Aaron shared with me that Pastor Wendell wanted me to come to the after-Fellowship Meeting and intimate group of pastors. As I entered the room, the guest speaker, Pastor Tommy Barnett, jumped up and gave me a handshake and said out loud to all the pastors that were in attendance, "This man has a heart to reach the forgotten people that are on the streets and all of you should get to know Pastor Ray Hampton, who's connected with the Dream Center in L.A. and who's Pastoring the Dream Center here in Seattle." As the night went on, I found myself sitting in the midst of greatness. By the time the after-fellowship was over Pastor Barnett had brought Pastor Wendell and I together and said, "I wonder what would happen if a suburban church that had the money linked up with an inner-city outreach ministry that is in the trenches. How powerful would that be?" At that moment my vision was coming clearer, I felt like singing the song, "I can see clearly now the rain is gone." After a successful unexpected meeting with Pastors Wendell and Tommy Barnett, two hours later I left and went home. As I was driving home, I was totally excited about what had just happened at the Church. I knew at this very moment that God was getting ready to expand the ministry again, but this time it was going to be something very special. Every morning and evening for the next couple of months, I couldn't get the meeting out of my mind no matter what I did. Finally, after the new year of 2003, I knew if I wanted to sleep, I had to be obedient to the Holy Spirit. Even though the Seattle International Church had moved multiple times, I felt again a tugging in my heart it was time to take another step.

23 The steps of a [good and righteous] man are directed and established by the LORD, And He delights in his way [and blesses his path].

Psalms 37:23 AMP

3 I knew that this was going to be hard for my family because of the multiple moves and we were starting to finally build some great relationship with the people of the church and community. One major thing that I have learned in ministry is that "People don't belong to the Pastor they belong to God". As a Pastor my assignment is to feed and equip the people for the work of the ministry. Also, to reproduce the kingdom by making Disciples!

Know and fully recognize with gratitude that the LORD Himself is God; It is He who has made us, not we ourselves [and we are His]. We are His people and the sheep of His pasture.

Psalms 100:3 AMP

"Then [in the final time] I will give you [spiritual] shepherds after My own heart, who will feed you with knowledge and [true] understanding.

Jeremiah 3:15 AMP

11 And [His gifts to the church were varied and] He Himself appointed some as apostles [special messengers, representatives], some as prophets [who speak a new message from God to the people], some as evangelists [who spread the good news of salvation], and some as pastors and teachers [to shepherd and guide and instruct], 12 [and He did this] to fully equip and perfect the saints (God's people) for works of service, to build up the body of Christ [the church].

Ephesians 4:11-12 AMP

[19] Go therefore and make disciples of all the nations [help the people to learn of Me, believe in Me, and obey My words], baptizing them in the name of the Father and of the Son and of the Holy Spirit.

Matthew 28:19 AMP

If you follow God's instructions for your life, He will always take care of you and your family, it does not matter if it is your biological or spiritual family. Well, the time of transition had finally come and by the third week of January, I made the announcement to the congregation that in two weeks, Seattle International Church will be connecting with The City Church in Kirkland, Washington. As you can already imagine, there were some excited people for the move, but there were some very upset people as well because this was all they knew, and they loved their church. I even remember one young man walking out of the sanctuary and went outside because he was so upset. Even though I had a straight face, inside my heart was hurting for him because it was not my intention to purposely hurt anyone. There are times in your life that you are going to face the same challenges, but always remember to listen and obey God's voice and to make the choice, God will always take care of everything.

27 The sheep that are My own hear My voice and listen to Me; I know them, and they follow Me.

John 10:27 AMP

In February of 2003, we finally began the journey of calling The City Church home, a few of the members even followed us there. While we were at the church, Pastor Wendel & Gini Smith scheduled a meeting to meet with my wife and I regarding the transition to make sure we were fine. There were a lot of great things that were spoken in the meeting regarding the present and future calling on our lives. One of the major things that I remember was when Pastor Wendell said that "Being at The City Church would be a time of nesting" for our family. I appreciate the love and concern that both of them had for our family, I remember them even paying some personal outstanding bills that were owed. Pastor Wendel & Gini even blessed us, personally giving us both what is known as a "Pentecostal Handshake" and the amount was liberating. Over the next eighteen months, I traveled across the country teaching and doing evangelism and outreach in many churches. Many doors continued to open for the Ray Hampton Outreach Ministries and relationship were built. The City Church were beginning to start satellite churches and Pastor Wendall had even spoke to me about the possibility of being a satellite pastor if they were blessed to find a downtown location. Many times, we drove throughout the inner-city of Seattle and downtown believing for a location. In June 2003, Pastor Wendell, myself and our wives took a trip to Los Angeles, California to attend the Los Angeles Dream Center Pastors and Leaders school and what a good time we had. After, one night of the school we all went out to dinner in Hollywood, California at the Hamburger Hamlett for fellowship. As we were having dinner, I felt honored to sit among such great men of God who were doing such amazing work in their city, state and around the world.

When we returned to Seattle, I continued to do outreach work throughout the city of Seattle. It was time for my favorite season of the year "Football." My sons, Ramon and Michael who played for Shorecrest High School had a Friday night game against Mariner High School at the shoreline stadium. As we were attending the game, a young boy walked up to me and said, "Is your name Ray Hampton?" and I said yes. As I was speaking, I recognized that the young boy was a son of the pastor of the church where I had served as pastor of evangelism from 1994-1997, It had been six years since I had seen Pastor Vince. As I went and greeted him in the stands, we both began to have a conversation regarding what had been going on within the last six years of our lives. I first shared with him how thankful I was for allowing me to serve as staff at Silver Lake Chapel and then I began to share with him how I had been traveling throughout the United States preaching and teaching the gospel. He asked me a question, "Are you also still feeding the hungry and homeless?" And I said of course that's the root of what I am called to do. I then asked him what new thing was going on in his life, he shared with me how the church was no longer located in Everett and had moved to downtown Seattle approximately ten months ago and how downtown needed a charismatic church. My response was, "wow.... that's awesome!" He also began to say that one of the main things that was lacking in the downtown was an out-reaching church that offered the basic necessities for the unlovely as well as items for families in need. The unique thing about this conversation was that I had been wanting to do a massive toy give away in a unique place and his facility perhaps could be the place. As we continued in conversation, he began to describe the building. Are you ready for this? It was a theatre that had a capacity to hold over one thousand people with plenty of parking places. Over the next month, after touring the facility the pastor said that he was going to take a vacation in the month of December as well as some ministry obligations and would I be available to speak for the month of December and that it was okay to use the facility for the toy giveaway. As we began to discuss the dates to preach on, I shared with him that the dates discussed were major dates for me for the month and since I was totally living from honorariums, love offerings to book sales, I needed to be available. We began to make plans to use the site for our "Christmas in the City" toy giveaway and in December 2003, Seattle International Church gave away over 10,0000 toys for Christmas, After all the years I had been around Pastor Tommy Barnett of Phoenix first Assembly of God and the Los Angeles International Dream Center, all I can still hear him say is (In that raspy voice); "There are three ways to know if you have a dream from God."

1. Is it bigger than you?
2. You cannot let it go.
3. What are you willing to give up to accomplish your dream?

When I thought about the challenge that was in front of me, it was not an interest it was an ultimate calling on my life and no matter what others thought about it, I knew I had to take a "step of faith"; I mean a "leap of faith."

22 Jesus replied, "Have faith in God [constantly].

Mark 11:22 AMP

11 Now faith is the assurance (title deed, confirmation) of things hoped for (divinely guaranteed), and the evidence of things not seen [the conviction of their reality—faith comprehends as fact what cannot be experienced by the physical senses].

Hebrews 11:1 AMP

The term leap of faith is a common idiom. To take a leap of faith means "to believe in something with no evidence for it" or "to attempt an endeavor that has little chance of success" to take a leap of faith is a metaphor for "belief in God.". Since we cannot observe God with our eyes, we must have faith that He is there. We jump from material concepts to the immaterial with a "leap of faith". Whenever you start to exercise your faith in God, it often requires you to take a risk.

> *7 for we walk by faith, not by sight [living our lives in a manner consistent with our confident belief in God's promises]*

2 Corinthians 5:7 AMP

A "Leap of Faith" is not a "Blind Leap of Faith". Our faith is backed by assurance and certainty and is supported by God's promises in His Word. A leap of faith is not an irrational impulse that causes you to jump out into the great unknown without any foresight. According to the word of God, born-again believers are to seek counsel from godly leaders.

> *14 Where there is no [wise, intelligent] guidance, the people fall [and go off course like a ship without a helm], But in the abundance of [wise and godly] counselors there is victory.*

Proverbs 11:14 AMP

> *"Without consultation and wise advice, plans are frustrated, but with many counselors they are established and succeed."*

Proverbs 15:22 AMP

22 *"Refuse good advice and watch your plans fail; take good counsel and watch them succeed."*

Proverbs 15:22 MSG

5-6 *"It's better to be wise than strong; intelligence outranks muscle any day. Strategic planning is the key to warfare; to win, you need a lot of good counsel."*

Proverbs 24:5-6 MSG

Chapter 9

THE KING CAT THEATRE

2004-2007

Now, I was getting ready to sign two leases on two buildings, one for $10,000 a month, which was the main building and $2500.00 a month for the children's church building which was located across the street. The church was located on the corner of 6th and Blanchard which was the last drop off for the free rides zone in downtown Seattle. So, that meant many people would be getting off right at the front door of our church and it also meant free advertisement to multiple people. Many people already knew about this location because before the previous church was there another business was there for years known as Jazz Alley which was and still is a very popular jazz and dinner venue in downtown Seattle. That very first year, the Seattle International Church experienced growth in the ministry not just physically, but financially. *(YouTube... Welcome to Seattle International Church and Dream Center)*

The church grew to over hundred and thirty members that year. I was no longer responsible for one staff member,

197

now I was responsible for multiple staff that had to be paid to run the organization successfully. In this thousand seat theater, the utility bills were almost three grand a month and with staff payroll and building lease, I was now looking at minimum of $19,000 every single month that I was responsible for; that is a lot of money for a congregation of 130 people, but I knew as long as I kept doing what God had called me to do that, He will continually see us through. Many great Outreach ministries were started that year, one that comes to mind was our sidewalk Sunday school where every Saturday we went to Yesler terrace low-income apartments to do a sidewalk Sunday school with the children. Once we arrived at Yesler terrace, the first thing that we did was clean up the area where we were going to have our sidewalk Sunday school. My wife Julia, who is the world's greatest children pastor I have ever known prepared her team to reach a harvest of children with excellence by presenting them the gospel through stories, games, puppet stage shows and so much more. Because of the drug activity that happens frequently in the area it was vitally important that we made sure the area was cleaned before the team began to minister. Once the area had been inspected, we were now ready to lay the giant tarp down on the ground for the children to sit on and set up the stage show with puppets and multiple games, food and prizes that was fun for the whole family.

Even though we did not have the funds to purchase buses and vans, we were able to charter a bus for five hours from the school district for $225 every single Sunday to go to the Yesler Terrace to pick up children and bring them to church on Sunday morning and believe me when I say the bus was full, it was full every Sunday!

Over the next couple of years, Seattle International Church continued to grow as we began to do daily commercials on television inviting people to church (*YouTube...Seattle International Church*).

Many National Football League (NFL) players of the Seattle Seahawks, such as Leonard Weaver, Marquis Weeks, Ray Willis, William Henry, Daryl Tapp, Floyd Womack, just to name a few, not just visited the church in downtown Seattle, but became acting members. Since 1999 we had given out thousands of toys every year, but 2006 was a transition year for our toy give away for Christmas. In October of that year, I was contacted by the Marines Toys 4 Tots about partnering with them to give away toys for Christmas. I was so excited about receiving the phone call that I was ready to jump up and scream. My question to the marines was, what initiated the phone call, and he began to explain to me that they were no longer giving toys to churches or other non-profits and we're now going to give to the Department of Social Health Service (DSHS) to give to families that are low income. As he continued to talk, the next words out of his mouth were, "Because the Seattle International Church and Dream Center has been so consistent in giving to the community for so many years, we figured that this would be a great partnership." As our conversation continued, we confirmed the pickup times to get the toys to give away for the upcoming toy giveaway. After multiple toy pickups, toy donations from our business site locations and from our Dream Center Partners, the number of toys collected were increasing daily. It was two weeks before Christmas and time for the volunteer staff to separate the toys. After a few days of toy separation, it was reported to me that we had collected over 22,000 toys from all donors. WOW! I knew that this was going to be a Christmas to Remember. Finally, the day had arrived for the giveaway, as over one-thousand people filled the Seattle International Church facility, which was over capacity in the sanctuary and even the foyer was filled with families waiting to receive the toys. Our musical production team who was led by Joanna Salomon was getting ready to start the musical "Emmanuel". This musical production was written and arranged by Joanna. She shared with me that this was the biggest attended crowd ever for "Emmanuel", so Joanna was very excited that so many people would be ministered to with the result that many would come to know Jesus. Joanna was right, when the altar call was made many people accepted Jesus into their life. Now, it was the time that everyone was waiting for, the toy giveaway. Before the toy giveaway started, the marines from "Toys 4 Tots" and multiple athletes from the Seattle Seahawks entered the stage and began to throw stuff animals into the audience. As they were throwing the stuff animals into the crowd, the volume became louder and louder from the shouts of the people. Once the crowd received multiple items, it was time for our production call "Emmanuel" which was a Christmas play written by our minister of music Joanna Salomon. The sanctuary and overflow were filled with over one thousand people who was anticipating what was going to happen. Everyone was directed to remain still as the lights dimmed throughout the sanctuary, the band began to play, and the actors began to enter not just on the stage, but from all over the sanctuary. The Emmanuel production lasted for approximately about two hours and immediately it was over the alter was full of people that wanted to receive Jesus in their life. After many people were prayed for and directed to go back to their seats; one of the Seattle International Staff noticed that there was water soaking an area of the sanctuary which eventually began to rapidly run throughout the church, but that did not stop what we were there to do, which was to give out thousands of toys to children. Minutes later I was notified that a water main on the outside of the building had burst. As the team continued to keep the area clean the people were directed to go out to the distribution area to receive multiple toys for their children. Channel 4 (KOMO News), Channel 5 (KING News) and Channel 7 (KIRO News) all reported that this was the largest gift distribution in King County. Check out the video of the toy gifts on: *YouTube "Seattle Dream Center Christmas in the City"*

As people flooded the toy distribution area, I was approached by one of our greeters and he shared with me that there was a man in the audience who wanted to meet with me the following week if my schedule allowed. I asked him to get his contact information and I will give him a call to schedule a meeting after the holidays, but I felt a strong urge from the Holy Spirit to meet with him at that moment. As I was introduced to him, he asked me a question, which was "Do you own this building?" My response was, "No, we don't own neither building, we are renting both for $12,500.00." The next question he asked me was an answer to our staff prayers. He shared with me that he wanted to make a financial donation of $200,000.00 designated to our building fund to purchase our own building. Even though I was on my way to have dinner with our guest, as you can imagine dinner was far from my mind at that moment; God was surely activating things in our ministry.

Chapter 10

THE MOVE TO WEST SEATTLE

2007-2010

On the first Sunday of January 2007, I announced to the congregation that we had received a $200,000.00 financial gift toward purchasing our own building to meet on Sundays, as well as continue our daily and weekly community and city outreach events. There was so much excitement in the auditorium that the place exploded with praise and worship, thanking God for what He has done! WOW.... If it had been any louder our congregation would have been on the local night news, responsible for causing an earthquake. That following week I contacted a Bank about purchasing a church building in West Seattle, which was going to be our first major purchase as a church. The building in West Seattle was absolutely amazing, it was located on a corner lot, 20,000 square feet of property with 13,000 square foot a building space three storeys high and overlooking alki beach for only $1.8 million dollars and it was absolutely beautiful. I knew deep down in my heart that this would be the right location for the Seattle International Church, and Dream Center to call home.

I was already imagining in my mind the world renown guest speakers that will come minister, the thousands of people that will come for our giveaways, thousands of salvations, water baptisms, marriages and families that were going to be restored, our annual community and city outreach, such as; Easter egg hunt, shoe giveaway, backpacks and school supply giveaway, Vacation Bible Adventure, Thanksgiving food giveaway, Christmas in the City Toy Giveaway and the list goes on. Once the meeting was scheduled at the bank, I could hardly wait for the day to come.

When the day of the meeting finally arrived, I was so excited! We met for over two and a half hours discussing the possibility of the purchase of the building in West Seattle for $1.8 million dollars, the lending director shared with me that it was tough to loan money to a church that was only three years old in its current location. I shared with him that we had $200,000 Dollars as a down payment. Because of the turnovers of Pastors in churches, at this time they did not want to take a chance on loaning a church any money. The bank informed me that I would need to come back and bring more money toward the down payment, so I asked them when we could meet again? They said, "the month of April will be a great month," which was only three months away. I was so frustrated about the Bank not loaning us the money that it made me even more determined to pursue not the building, but the promise God had for us. it was very important at this moment that I had to stay not point focused, but aim focused on what the word of God said in the following scripture.

6 "Do not be anxious or worried about anything, but in everything [every circumstance and situation] by prayer and petition with thanksgiving, continue to make your [specific] requests known to God."

Philippians 4:6 AMP

I knew that God was doing something behind the scenes for Seattle International Church. I felt in my heart that God was setting up something great and so, I immediately went to the congregation the following week. As I began to speak on that Sunday morning, I shared with the congregation that we were going to do an impact giving over the next three months. Everybody was asked to bring $1000 over and above their tithes and offering by or on April 8, which was Easter Sunday morning. On the following morning when the staff had returned to the office, they began to count the tithes, offering and the Impact contributions that were collected. Later that morning the total contributions were reported to my office. Not only was the amount of our tithes and offerings in the thousands, which was amazing, but once the finance team had shared with me what the impact giving was it was absolutely incredible! Are you ready for this? The total impact contributions were over $52,830. WOW!

I was so excited to know that the Seattle International Church members were totally invested into the vision. The most amazing thing about the Impact giving was, that between January and April the Seattle International Church members were still consistent in their tithes and offering. On Sunday April 15th, when the announcement was made of the total amount of the Impact giving, if you thought that the announcement of the $200,000 was explosive, you should have heard the noise that took place once the impact total was announced. It was louder than the fans at the Seahawk Football Stadium.

A week later I contacted the same bank to let them know about the amount of the Impact giving and wanted to set up another meeting with them. When I told them the amount of the Impact giving, they were in total shock that a church of our size could raise such a large amount in a short time and still maintain our monthly expenses. The vice president of commercial lending even made a comment and said, "Your $52,000 that was raised is an average of almost $17,000 a month and that is absolutely incredible". He also said, "We have been in discussion about you for the last three months since our last meeting and would like to talk to you further once we meet." Before our phone conversation was over a meeting was scheduled for the following week. The days and nights couldn't come fast enough before the meeting could take place. Finally, the time came for us to meet and when I walked into their office, I felt a calmness in the atmosphere. As the meeting started, the financial lender just shouted out and said, "I'm just going to get to why we are here and give you the great news. We are going to loan you the $1.8 million dollars to purchase your new church building." I remember shouting out! Really, are you serious? One of the men that represented the Commercial lending team said, "yes, we are very serious." At that moment, I asked them what the next steps were, and the response was, all you need to do is take this packet with you to your office and go over it with your team and once everything is approved and signed, we'll set up another meeting with your team to go over the documents.

Still in shock, I ask the following question, "What was the change of mind, is it because we were now able to put a $252,000 down payment". Their response was, "the down payment is a tremendous help and we applaud your church for their effort to make it happen." They continued to explain to me one after another that over the last three months they decided to do a background check on me to find out more about our history in non-profit. During their findings they saw that for almost the last 20 years that I have been serving disadvantaged people from Everett to Seattle by providing food, clothes, shelter, and many other things. "…We figured that anyone that has been this consistent and mobile for all these years deserves to have a place to call home, so we want to offer you the loan "based on a character reference." The next words that came out of my mouth was, "Thank You!"

When the meeting ended, I left the property excitedly that as I was driving, I continued to give God praise all the way home. One of the major reasons that I was so excited is because two weeks before this meeting I was turned down for a third cell phone line at sprint, but now I was approved for a $1.8 million dollar loan not only that, but I began to reminisce how thirteen years before this I was on section 8 (Government Housing), but now I'm receiving a loan on a character reference. Maybe one day I'll write a book on how to go from "Section 8 to 1.8". I even remember that at the same time we were on section 8 receiving welfare every month. Just in case you are wondering what welfare is. The new name is called E.B.T, but the welfare that I'm talking about is the food stamp books that look like monopoly money, but its spendable. But now I'm getting 1.8 million dollars on a character reference to purchase a building. Sounds like another book that I can write by flipping the word welfare around and giving the book the title "Farewel to welFare".

Finally, the papers were signed to purchase our "New church building" in west Seattle and the monthly payment to be an owner versus a renter was better than what we were currently paying. Before, we were at $12,500 a month as renters and now, we are owners of our own property and paying $9056.23 every month. Many people gave financially to our church to help us to continue to make a great impact in the city. One person that stands out is a great friend of mine named Todd Quinn. One morning I received a phone call from his office that he wanted to meet with me regarding our outreaches throughout the city. The following week, his administrator himself and I met at the Huckleberry in Burien, Washington for breakfast. As we were discussing the possibility about partnering together, he jumped up and said, "I'll be back." When he returned into the restaurant, he had a folded check in his hand. As Todd handed me the envelope he said, "open it up". I couldn't believe what I was seeing, a check for $10,000 to put in the outreach account. Todd continued to say, "the next time you will see a check; it will have another" "0", it would be for $100,000!" I've eaten many breakfasts at home and at restaurants, but that morning the corn beef hash, soft scramble eggs, fried potatoes, two pancakes and a large orange juice was the best breakfast I have ever eaten in my life. There was another time when Todd called the church office and asked to speak to RayRay I remember the office administrator saying, "we don't have a RayRay that works here". Todd said, "okay then, can I speak to Pastor RayRay?" I'll never forget the expression on her face. Once Todd was connected to me, he said, "Do you have any outstanding bills that need to be paid at the Church?" My response was, "yes, the basic utilities and phone bill etc." Todd then asked me to have my office tally up all outstanding bills and send it to Him. Well, guess what happened? A week later, my daughter Catrena and I met Todd at the South Center Mall in Tukwila, Washington and he handed me an envelope for over $5,300 to pay every outstanding bill. I will always be grateful to Todd for his prayers and financial generosity!

Many conferences also took place in the building and many guest speakers from across the United States, such as Drs. Mike & DeDe freeman, Jamaal Bryant, Canton Jones, and Tim Storey and Casey Treat, just to name a few.

Chapter 11

THE MOVE TO SOUTH SEATTLE

2010-2016

Because of the need of many individuals and families that lived across the west Seattle bridge leading into south Seattle, I decided to open a second location for Seattle International Church in the skyway at the Lakeridge Elementary School to start having another service. Our West Seattle campus time was at 10:00 am and the south campus starting time was at 1:00pm. What an adjustment it was for our staff, such as the praise and worship team, children and youth workers, office, and pastoral team. Preparation and timing were very important every Sunday to meet the needs in both cities. Skyway where the church was located was an unincorporated city that is located in king county, and it was known as a city between two cities". At the time of this writing, to my knowledge, skyway is still an unincorporated city located between two cities, Renton, and Seattle. Skyway as a city was experiencing a lot of crime and many people were moving out of the community, but others could not afford to move. Skyway was a city that had two busy casinos, a few hair salons, corner stores, a barbeque, a restaurant, chicken restaurant, eleven churches and a grocery outlet store that used to be an old vacant building.

I remember one day walking into grocery outlet to purchase some items and as I was paying for my items, I was approached by one of the cashiers who knew that the Seattle international church and Dream Center over the last twenty years was responsible for a lot of major outreaches throughout the city of Seattle. The next question she asked me was, "Have you ever approached the owners about partnering together to change lives in skyway by making an impact through the vehicle of outreach?" Over the next few weeks, I was in meetings with the owners to help them in their community outreach efforts by inviting people throughout the community to come show case their talents, on a stage they had built on the property. There was also a gas station located across the street where I approached the owner about giving away free gas to everyone that was in need and five months later, we were able to have our outreach called "Meet me at the pump".

We put five dollars' worth of gasoline in over one-Hundred cars. Also, the outreach team offered each person(s) in the car prayer for any request and of course, we prayed with them the prayer of salvation and the response was great, they were also given a bible and invitation to Seattle International Church.

Our "Back 2 School Giveaway" was another amazing outreach where we gave away thousands of backpacks filled with school supplies to children throughout the Renton and Seattle School District. One year we even adopted the Lakeridge Elementary School to make sure that every child had what was needed, so they could start off the school year on a positive note. After years of giving thousands of backpacks filled with school supplies to families in need, and providing the same items to children, such as churches, schools, professional athletes, and organizations it was time to make a shift and add to what we were offering to the children to prepare them to go back to school. Are you ready for this? As a team, we decided to give away shoes to the children at the "Kickn it back to school" Shoe Outreach. Now that we had the name, it was time to go get the shoes and to my amazement just like every other outreach many people started to respond, such as our local church (Seattle International Church), the committed individuals on our mailing list and local business owners. Not to leave out anyone because every person and business that provided either shoes or finances to the outreach was responsible in making a huge impact in a child's life, but I would like to take this time to highlight a couple of businesses. Ezell's Fried Chicken owners Lewis and Jackie Rudd were just amazing. They wanted to make sure that every volunteer staff member and all the families that attended the event did not leave hungry. Ezell's provided hundreds of pieces of spicy and original chicken, rolls, barbecue bake beans and Cole Slaw for everyone! Another year, Popeyes chicken Owner gave $1000.00 toward the outreach and Vanessa Ellis, the operations manager for the organization even allowed customers to give to the cause in all of her (Popeyes) stores throughout the state of Washington. That year in our shoe outreach give away, we gave away three-hundred and thirty-six pairs of shoes and from that starting point we are still giving away shoes till today! To see videos of the outreaches, you can see it in action on you tube or go to the following web site (Put YouTube link name here) To date we have given away 746 pairs of brand-new shoes to children for school.

From a few years of meeting in a school gymnasium, we had an opportunity to move into a church facility as shared space with the Lakeridge Lutheran Church where we were able not only to continue all our outreaches, but add additional outreaches to the community and one of those were the summer feeding program.

One Day at my office I received a phone call from United Way of King County, they wanted to partner with the Seattle International Dream Center to help feed hungry children in unincorporated south king county (Skyway), and decided that our organization would be a great fit because of the amount of media attention we were receiving due to our free weekly

,monthly and annual community give aways. Of course, I said yes and two weeks later we were given a $3500.00 dollar check for transportation to give out food every day for two months. What an amazing summer to see children eat lunch together and build relationships in a safe environment while many parents were at work trying to provide for their family.

The church's last move was to the Rainier Beach Community Center where again we partnered with the community center to host all of the outreaches on site, this was so amazing to me because the center was already offering sport clinics and swimming to low-income families. Our partnership with the Rainier beach community center was perfect. The first giveaway, another shoe giveaway on site brought in hundreds of children. Panda Express catered the event for free, providing a huge buffet of food for everyone. Even though our church had moved eight locations throughout the years, the heart to serve others never changed as the outreaches continued to grow larger and larger. We always remained "In the heart of the city, with the city in our hearts." For the first twenty-five years and counting, many of the outreaches are still being offered to City of Seattle and the surrounding areas,

A lot of giveaway outreaches were done from our south Seattle location!

Backpack and school supplies:

YouTube...2010 Backpack Giveaway

Gas Giveaway:

YouTube...2010 Meet Me At The Pumps

YouTube...Meet me at the pump Gas Give Away

YouTube...Gas Give Away in Skyway

Toy Giveaway:

YouTube...Seattle International Church Toy Giveaway

YouTube...Seattle Dream Center Toy Give Away Ray Hampton

22,000 Toys The largest toy giveaway in King County

YouTube...Seattle Dream Center Christmas in the City

Free Lunch for Children in the Summer:

YouTube...Seattle International Church and Dream Center summer feeding to Children

YouTube...Feeding free lunch to children for the summer

Mobile Library to go for Children:

YouTube...Seattle International Church and Dream Center bringing the library to the feeding summer lunch outreach

Over 1,000 people attended Liberty Park in Renton, Washington to hunt for over 15,000 Plastic Eggs

filled with Candy (Largest Egg Hunt in King County) :

YouTube…Seattle International Church prepares for Egg Hunt at Liberty Park in Renton, Washington

YouTube… Seattle International Church Flashlight Egg Hunt at Liberty Park in Renton, Washington **Part 1**

YouTube… Seattle International Church Flashlight Egg Hunt at Liberty Park in Renton, Washington **Part 2**

YouTube… Seattle International Church Flashlight Egg Hunt at Liberty Park in Renton, Washington **Part 3**

Feeding the Homeless and Hungry:

YouTube…Seattle International Church feeding the hungry in Downtown Seattle

"Taking it to the Streets" is about the first twenty-five years of ministry (1991-2016). Ray Hampton Outreach Ministries is not just headquartered on the West Coast in Seattle, Washington, but now has expanded to its second headquarters on the East Coast in Fort Lauderdale, Florida. Dr. Ray Hampton is a consultant to hundreds of churches and non-profits across the United States teaching, how to engage, be equipped and empowered for evangelism and outreach. In the first five years (2016-2021) in Fort Lauderdale, Florida, Ray Hampton Outreach Ministries has been able to make a major impact in the surrounding cities, at their Each One Reach One

217

outreach events. Over 336 Hygiene packs to the homeless has been given out, 843 Cars have received free gas, over 10,859 plastic eggs filled with candy at a community easter egg hunt, 1,298 Backpacks filled with School supplies and over 11,515 toys have been given out to children for Christmas, just to name a few achievements.

The year was July 1991; at the age of twenty-six, Dr. Ray Hampton realized he had a passion to help people in a great way, so he went out on the street corner to start feeding the homeless and hungry. It was at that moment that Ray Hampton Outreach Ministries was started. Dr. Ray is now an entrepreneur, television personality, public figure, and author. He also serves as an evangelism and outreach church growth consultant to many churches throughout the United States teaching people the rules of engagement, equipping, and empowering them for evangelism and outreach.

Dr. Ray is a mentor to many people, like, National Football League players, chief executive officers, and leaders. He believes in higher education, having started at Washington State University, and continued his education at A. L. Hardy Academy of Theology. To his acclaim, he currently holds a master's degree in marriage and biblical family counseling and two doctoral degrees, one in ministry and the other in theology. Dr. Hampton currently lives in Fort Lauderdale, Florida, with his wife, Julia whom he married at seventeen years old. They have been married for thirty-nine years and raised ten children. Over 103,852 toys have been distributed to children for Christmas,16,490 backpacks filled with school supplies and hundreds of thousands of meals have been provided to individuals and families experiencing food insecurities. These are just a few of the major outreaches that have had an impact on people's lives. He continues to provide answers to problems by serving with his palms down and not his palms up.